BEAUTY BY DESIGN

REFRESHING SPACES
INSPIRED BY
WHAT MATTERS MOST

FOUNDER OF

GINGER CURTIS

HARVEST HOUSE PUBLISHERS
EUGENE, OREGON

dedicate this book to
my amazing team now
and over the years. From our earliest projects as emerging designers to our current
achievements as an established firm, these
professional women have shaped who we are
and been foundational in our success. I have cried many tears
on their shoulders, celebrated huge triumphs, and absolutely
everything in between. They have lifted me up when I thought
I couldn't press on, and they have been my colleagues as well as my dear
friends. Their loyalty, dedication, ingenuity, and insane talent have inspired
me on a daily basis. Martina, Melissa, Marian, Fatima, Amanda, and Liz, you
have been and are the *best* part of my job!

   And to my husband, Eric, and my sister, Cindy. Your endless love and support have helped me weather the storms and claim new courage to tackle
my dreams.

   I love you.

✕ CONTENTS

A NEW BEAUTY EMERGES

Every time I host a project tour live on Instagram, share a post of my red-haired, snuggly little ones assisting me in the kitchen, or take my followers into the homes of my design clients, I'm welcoming everyone to the most intimate parts of my life and the inspirations for my work. Sharing what matters most is my biggest privilege and blessing. Even when I didn't run my own design firm or have my own house, I understood the power of beauty to nourish and heal hearts, bodies, and spirits.

I've always desired to create a sense of comfort in the spaces around me. I found small ways to do this for my sisters and brothers and myself when my childhood home was a place of abuse and neglect. I was the second oldest of seven kids born to a father who was physically and emotionally abusive and a mom who struggled to parent us while she too was stuck in a cycle of control.

We fiercely looked after each other. I made it my role to bring love and beauty into my siblings' lives in whatever way I could. Knowing that dinner for the seven of us would be prepared from a single box of macaroni and cheese, I set the table with place mats, cups, and silverware to give my family the security and comfort of being cared for. I created order wherever possible—making my bed, helping my mom with the laundry, and showing my siblings how to keep their spaces neat— hoping to usher in a sense of stability and joy amid uncertainty. We moved from a run-down apartment to a run-down house while our dad worked in a variety of sales jobs. When I was ten, my dad's career stabilized, and my parents bought a two-story home in a suburban development in Fort Worth. I had my own bedroom for the very first time, and I couldn't wait to make it my refuge.

I did everything I could to hang on to the privilege of enjoying that sweet space. I watched my mom be creative with very little and find ways to refresh areas of the home, so I did the same in my little sanctuary. Each morning after rising, I made my bed with care, folding the top sheet and comforter just so, smoothing away any wrinkles, and then carefully arranging all my pillows before adding the throw blanket at the foot of the bed. If a sibling wanted to push my buttons, they would hurl themselves onto my bed and mess up that day's creation of beauty and order.

After school, I hurried back to my room, where I would continue to plan, create, and dream. This was when I first experienced the healing power of beautiful spaces and discovered that a home can express contentment and happiness—and safety.

When my father put us in harm's way, I retreated to my refuge and calmed myself by singing the hymns we learned in church. I communed with the Lord, feeling protected, defended, and cherished. It still moves me deeply to know that in that sparse, tiny room, God was preparing me for how he wanted to use my life.

In time, my father became a man of committed faith and love. He has received my forgiveness, and God has restored our relationship. Redemption is the ultimate emergence of beauty from brokenness. In the decades that followed my childhood, I

watched God continue to work through my love of home to show others how worthy they are of his goodness. I'm created to host a meal for people who need a table to gather round. I'm designed to build a piece of furniture from discarded items to make our house feel like home. I'm shaped to help other people's hopes become reality.

My business, Urbanology Designs, exists today because of the desires planted in a young girl's heart. And this book exists because those desires continue to bloom to encourage you to find beauty and strength in your everyday life.

Walk Through the Door

From day one, I wanted my business to be personal. And what is more personal than joining an individual or family on a tour of their sanctuary while discovering ways to make that space even more fully "them"? I started offering a service to clients called a walk-through. We pick a day for me to show up and journey through their home as they open doors, drapes, and closets so I can better understand their needs. I take it all in with joy. I ask them questions about light, color, and style likes and dislikes as we walk from room to room. I share what a sense of home has meant to me from childhood and through the years, and they open up about what matters most to them. Sometimes they apologize because belongings are scattered on the floor or the living room has furniture they purchased on impulse but have never embraced. I'm quick to reassure them that they never need to apologize for anything. Areas in which we hope to improve exist inside our four walls and inside ourselves. Every day we have the opportunity to embrace and celebrate the beauty our homes and lives are designed to express.

Regardless of what life might throw at us, this journey is about noticing the new beauty emerging in your challenges and trials, your detours and dreams. Start watching for it.

New beauty emerges in our hopes and plans.

New beauty emerges in our priorities and foundations.

THIS JOURNEY IS ABOUT NOTICING THE NEW BEAUTY EMERGING IN YOUR CHALLENGES AND TRIALS, YOUR DETOURS AND DREAMS.

New beauty emerges in our faith and patience.

New beauty emerges in the grandest vision and the smallest detail.

In the lives of women, there's so much to manage, figure out, and deal with. But one of the greatest insights that my life and profession have taught me is this: Just as great design is not created in a single decision but by bringing many wonderful details together, life is not defined by one or two huge decisions as much as it is shaped by daily details. By tending to our homes and families and investing in our dreams and priorities, we can cultivate the beauty we desire.

I've written this to encourage you through your own transformation. I structured the chapters around the concepts that I believe are most important in design and in our lives. From foundational elements to fun accessories and one-of-a-kind touches, we'll talk about it all.

The best part of all this is that whatever your level of design experience or your need might be, you can experiment and have fun with these principles. To personalize this adventure, I include a walk-through moment with each chapter that I hope will serve you right where you are. Concept by concept we will explore your spaces and your hopes as we connect in our homes and our hearts. This is a journey that will surprise and delight you from the moment we walk through the door, ready to see beauty.

Let's get started—so much possibility awaits.

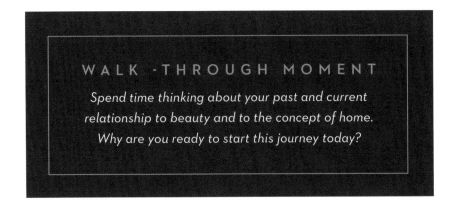

WALK ·THROUGH MOMENT

Spend time thinking about your past and current relationship to beauty and to the concept of home. Why are you ready to start this journey today?

PART ONE

—————

DREAM

OF

BEAUTY

ONE

YOU'RE WORTHY OF BEAUTY

magine. Dream. Expand those horizons.

Spend time with your head in the clouds while you wander the stretch of possibility from your entryway to your back door. Or fill a favorite mug with peppermint tea, settle into a cozy chair next to a big basket of design magazines and books, and dive in to discover what a room could become.

These are a couple of wonderful ways to move toward preparing your home for beautiful change. However, neither of them is the *key* first step. The first step is *believing that you're worthy*.

Some women have that nailed; they've learned over time and from special mentors, godly teachers, and heart-friends that they are worthy to dream and invest in beauty and who they are becoming. Others feel like it's taking a lifetime to reach a place of belief. This is necessary for any kind of change to unfold, whether it's a renovation inside a home or an upgrade in our lives. Take a rich moment to ask yourself and answer this question: Do you believe you are worthy?

Well, here's the truth . . .

You are worthy of beauty.

I know that. God knows that. Do *you* know that?

You are worthy of experiencing beauty, creating it, appreciating it, and leaning into it during good times and times of difficulty.

Craving Beauty

I have discovered that many of my clients initially reach out to me during or after seasons of unrest, transition, or loss. It makes sense that we crave replenishment and are ready to dream after we've been depleted by the desert times of our journey.

I am programmed to dream big when circumstances are difficult. So when my family entered the desert, I responded by *remodeling our entire house.*

My son Asher was just five months old when I felt the lump in my breast.

The diagnosis was the most aggressive type of breast cancer, with a high proliferation rate because all the estrogen and progesterone during my pregnancy had fed the cancer. Just months before, we'd come through my young daughter Avery's treatment for leukemia, and now, for the first time, I wasn't stepping up and fighting for someone else. This was my life . . . and I was scared.

That is when God invited me to begin a new path of healing through beauty.

My husband, Eric, takes a personal sabbatical each year during which he goes away to be with God alone and pray. This time he returned with a very clear impression on his heart—it was time to look for a bigger home. My heart leapt at the possibility of an adventure. Yes! We got into search mode and quickly found a larger home mere blocks away that needed TLC and extra portions of elbow grease. The deal went through. I couldn't wait to get started.

The selling residents kindly allowed me to come to the house six weeks before our move-in day so I could take measurements and

If it is a woman's nature to nurture,
then she must nourish herself.

ANNE MORROW LINDBERGH

photos. Sometimes I would stare at a space until I had a vision. They may have thought I was crazy, but they must have also felt bad for the bald woman walking around with a tape measure, because they pretty much let me do whatever I needed.

When we were finally able to move in, I was in the middle of chemo, I was nurturing our baby, and I was healing from a mastectomy. My body was weak, my hair gone, and my immune system stripped down. But everything inside me told me to create. Without hesitation, I rolled up my sleeves and started tearing out cupboards and flooring. I continued staring into spaces to see what was possible and what suited the needs and hopes of our family.

I hired builders to tackle projects requiring know-how I didn't have or physical strength well beyond what my frail body could muster (even with the force of my notable stubbornness behind it!). Some early mornings, a crew was already in the kitchen working when I, with my scarf-covered head, made my weary way down our staircase, step by slow step. They would turn and watch me, holding their breath. I'm sure they fought the urge to just pick me up and carry me down to assure my safe passage between our two floors. By this time, they knew I would refuse offers of assistance. I wanted to find my way. I wanted to feel what was happening—not the pain or the worry; I wanted to feel and follow the incredible momentum toward beauty.

Mind you, this was before Urbanology Designs came into existence. The people around me thought I was absolutely nuts. Every couple of days, poor Eric would field yet another phone call from someone who was kindly but firmly telling him that his wife really should be lying in bed drinking juice and resting and not going all HGTV in every room of our simple two-story house.

But my kindhearted, wise husband knew me, and he trusted what God was doing in me. Through this, the Lord faithfully renewed my spirit. In my weakness, he provided strength. I was soft worn. Durable. Not indestructible, but willing to withstand. The light and determination that grew in me during this period in my life would

CREATING A

SANCTUARY

FOR

YOURSELF,

FAMILY,

AND OTHERS

IS SACRED

WORK.

permeate every aspect of who I was. Through yet one more great hardship, God was designing something spectacular.

This soft-worn durability would become my design style and the style in which I work in others' lives. It is my trademark because what God would produce out of this sickness would become the miracle that would define me as the woman I am today.

Start Dreaming

Your home is your own little world, and it's a space that ultimately reflects who you are. And who you are is a beautiful combination of the way God made you *and* what you've done with the life you've been given. What you've been through will infuse and fuel your dreams for your family, yourself, and the place that gives you shelter and joy.

What dream might be unfolding for you right now? What is your dream for your home? I have clients who delayed moving forward for a long time because they could not give themselves permission to consider their surroundings worth the investment. On the other hand, they would immediately tell a friend she deserves to create a bedroom that inspires her.

By the way, when I say investment, I don't mean money. You might choose to set aside funds or save over time to pursue bigger design and architectural changes or to invite newer pieces of furniture into your home. That's all fine—and incredibly fun. But women often don't feel worthy of investments of time, attention, and care toward anything that nurtures them back.

We often pour into other people's lives. But to pause and find ways to create spaces and opportunities that refill *us*—that can initially feel uncomfortable. (This too shall pass!) Also, we can mistakenly believe the only tasks that are holy are the grand gestures of faith or service. But the Lord designed each of us to enjoy beauty, to appreciate magnificence. It's in my DNA, it's in your DNA—and honey, just own it. Creating a sanctuary for yourself, family, and others is sacred work.

Be still in your space and spend time reflecting on your journey.

Express your dreams. Say those lovelies aloud, tell friends about them, write them down.

Ask someone in your life to share insight and encouragement about you and your dream.

Understand the value of what you have to offer through your heart and home.

Take time to plan a next step or two or four. Use this book to keep going.

Yes. Say it. Yes, you have permission to foster the beauty you long for.

That's why letting yourself dream is a crucial starting place. May beauty lead you to inspiration and permission to dream.

Put a date on the calendar for a personal walk-through of your home. Sit in each space and think about what your dream for that room, nook, or area is. Do some sitting and staring to see what picture unfolds.

Not everyone is visual, which is why a little later we'll explore other ways to identify your hope and purpose for your home. If no design or decor images came to mind as you went through each room, consider whether you saw glimpses of how you, your family, and others use and enjoy a room. That's the perfect start to a dream.

Dreams Bloom in All Circumstances

When I was three-quarters of the way through chemo and mostly done designing our home renovation, Eric and I hosted a life group from church in our remodeled living room. One of our friends offered up a question as an icebreaker: "What would you do with your life if you could do anything?" Answers began to pop around the room with bursts of laughter.

"I'd be a ballerina!"

"I'd race cars!"

I waited for my turn to come around, astonished that I had never asked myself that question. I thought of all the moments in my past that made me feel the happiest. I realized that my greatest pleasure has always come from creating surroundings to make others feel loved and special. If I could do anything...really? *Anything*?

"I'd start my own design firm!" The words tumbled out, yet they were clear with conviction. That idea had never been in my mind before, yet the Lord had used every moment in my life up to then to make my calling clear *right in that moment.*

As surprised as I was to speak those words aloud, all the people around me nodded. They weren't shocked at all. In recent years, they all had witnessed my abilities and watched God shape my talents to serve in this way.

A few days later, I received an invitation from a friend's mother, who was a designer, to help her stage a home to sell. Instantly my passion went into high gear. I had so many ideas. I only made a few bucks on that first staging, but Eric and I looked at each other as if to say, "It's raining money!"

By the time I finished that first project, I had established a business and filed for an LLC—and likely shocked my husband. The inspiration I felt made it so clear this was where God wanted me to go. The best part was that it was always in me. I was just stepping up to take on what God wanted me to do next. There's a Bible verse— Romans 8:28—that expresses this well: "We know that in all things

God works for the good of those who love him, who have been called according to his purpose." God had taken my life—broken, hurting, and not working—and totally repurposed it.

God is the author of creativity and beauty, of order and harmony. During that difficult and exciting year, he spoke to my heart: "You had the faith to walk through your past—and now you have a future of giving hope and beauty to others."

Regardless of what you have been through or the condition of your surroundings right now, there is an "after" just up ahead. In fact, you and I might walk through more than a couple of those in this journey together. You, my friend, are worthy of your "after."

WALK-THROUGH MOMENT

What dream for your home is rising? Do you feel worthy to embark on this journey of beauty?

TWO

SET PRIORITIES AND PLUMB LINES

believe the environment we live in has a strong emotional impact on us and everyone who crosses our threshold—little kiddos, extended family, friends, fellowship groups, or the neighbor you've lived by for eight years and only got to know recently when you finally invited her to come over.

It's time for us to reconnect with the sense of home that echoed loudly in past generations. To once again enjoy moments of "come over to my porch and have lemonade while we shoot the breeze." Let's offer our friends a spur-of-the-moment invitation, just as they are and just as we are, to join us for dinner or a dessert night and games. Imagine reclaiming the influence of our homes on the lives around us, the communities we live in, and the world beyond our spot on the map. We can believe in that, and we can treat our four walls like they are giving shelter to love, hope, faith, and charity.

The old saying "charity begins at home" is about caring first for the people in your immediate circle. Let's reframe that phrase: Home is where the heart of charity begins. Our homes are the sources, the wells where we and others fill up, become encouraged, understand strengths and gifts, and manifest beauty that emerges within and is then shared with those outside our walls.

This time of taking stock can be life changing, friend. Let's not miss this opportunity.

Let's start with identifying what you want people to feel the moment they enter your home. When I ask clients this question, their first response often goes something like this: "I don't want my home to feel precious. I want it to feel livable. Real." This is universally important. However, the ways we turn our home into a space that is welcoming and real will vary greatly. The interior design of our lives—the way God made us—will impact our hopes, priorities, and goals for the interior design of our homes.

This next exercise will draw you closer to what suits you and your personal interior design. Here is a list of some emotions and feelings. Take time to read through it and note those that represent what you want your home to offer someone the moment they walk in. This is a first-impression feeling. Later we will talk about the mood of a home—the lasting impression, the look and ambience that sustains a feeling in your home.

ACCEPTANCE	ENERGY	HAPPINESS	POSITIVITY
AFFECTION	ENCOURAGEMENT	INSPIRATION	RELAXATION
BLESSING	ENTHUSIASM	JOY	SAFETY
CALM	EXCITEMENT	LOVE	STRENGTH
CHEERFULNESS	FREEDOM	MOTIVATION	SURPRISE
CONTENTMENT	GRATEFULNESS	OPTIMISM	WELCOME
DELIGHT	HOPEFULNESS	PLEASURE	

Life's a voyage that's
homeward bound.

HERMAN MELVILLE

Are there other feelings you want your home to evoke? Create your own list in a home journal or design notebook.

Exploring which feelings you want to evoke in your home helps you identify your priorities and your personal style. When you embrace authenticity, inspiration follows. This is what I help my clients achieve when I work with them to redesign their homes—and I hope to help you do the same. Each understanding leads to insight for the next stage of the process.

Focus on What Matters Most

When I was ambling about our new-to-us home during my chemo treatments and clarifying my vision, I knew a priority for this home would be to bless my family and others and to use it to honor God.

I went through the same process when I started Urbanology Designs. I had an LLC established, a big dream floating in my head, a business plan to fine tune, and a small room in our house to claim as my office. I quickly articulated my reason, my mission statement for this passion pursuit, and it nearly echoed my purpose for my home: to be a blessing to my family and to use my gifts to honor God.

I could hold up each business decision to this and see if it lined up with my priorities and purpose. I was a new business owner juggling multiple clients and handling every aspect of the work. Every day presented decisions, some that were simple and in the moment, and others that were more complex with long-term implications. As the business quickly grew, I hired three employees. They shared that small home office with me. Initially, this was great. I was available to my family and to my clients. I had the freedom to pause work and go pick up one of the girls. I could wander upstairs anytime to check in with the kids or help them with homework.

But after some time and some business growth, Eric and I discussed whether this arrangement was becoming too disruptive. The answer was yes. The work and the business honored God, but using a home office for a growing staff was no longer a blessing to my family.

THE INTERIOR
DESIGN OF
OUR LIVES—
THE WAY GOD
MADE US—
WILL IMPACT
OUR HOPES,
PRIORITIES,
AND GOALS
OF THE
INTERIOR
DESIGN OF
OUR HOMES.

By clarifying my priorities for my home space and my professional calling, I was accountable and encouraged to be unwavering. Such a gift of protection! The same statement remains my guide and guardrail. Eric and I refer to it to protect our family, set our plans, inform our prayers, and weigh decisions to be sure they line up with what matters most.

I encourage clients to understand their why, their goals...their plumb line. In construction, a plumb line is a string with a weight at the end. It hangs straight down and shows you whether a wall or post or whatever is true. Our family uses the words and promises of God as our plumb line to set our priorities in all areas of life.

Whether you are taking on a project yourself or hiring professionals, the plumb line will help you make decisions and remember why you started in the first place. Believe me, we all need those reminders occasionally, regardless of how large or small our projects.

Have you ever emptied out a hall closet to organize it, only to find yourself sitting on the floor with stuff on all sides and a deep desire to cry or go take a nap because you're overwhelmed? Starting by stating your mission will help: *I want to organize this closet to get rid of what I don't need and to have easy access to what I do need.* You'll be glad for this clear statement when frustration tempts you to quit for the day and shove everything back before anyone knows what you had aspired and failed to do. The plumb-line statement behind this mission might be to care about people more than you care about things.

Think through these questions to identify your plumb line (your guide and measure) and your mission statement (your goal in a specific life area). Talk with your family to better understand their thoughts about your home environment. They might mention something you hadn't thought of.

What inspires you?

What do you value?

What makes you feel good?

What do you want others to feel as they enter your home?

What is your core purpose for your home?

What are your immediate family members' desires for your home?

When difficulties arise, what goal will keep you going?

I want you to feel inspired every day by your surroundings. My hope is that you will love your home so much you'll see it as a sanctuary. And that it will fill and refresh you like your favorite vacation place. I pray this journey will help you create a life and environment that you love and that serves others in whatever ways you are called to share.

WALK-THROUGH MOMENT

What emotions do you want your home to evoke? What is your plumb-line statement? Write this down in your home journal or design notebook.

THREE

DISCOVER WHAT YOU LOVE

A space at its best reflects what you love, not what you are told to treasure. Something unexpected and magnificent happens when you let go of perfection and embrace creativity and authenticity. At Urbanology Designs, we are committed to this unfussy yet elegant approach to design. The moment we express it to clients, they breathe a sigh of relief. Chances are, they've been trying to model their efforts on someone else's version of beauty, and they've become frustrated because nothing quite feels right. Maybe they duplicated a look from a magazine and put it in their home without modifying it for their needs, their aesthetic, their home's challenges and blessings.

Break away from rules to create an inspiring, pulled-together look that reflects the best of who you are. Give yourself permission to build on knowing you are worthy of beauty and worthy of creating a home that reflects that beauty. Don't get hung up on what anyone else thinks, expects, or is doing.

EACH OF

US HAS A

UNIQUE STYLE

BECAUSE

EACH OF US

HAS A UNIQUE

STORY.

Before you start a design project, it is good to recognize your style. What do you like enough to invite into your home for an extended stay? This can be a stumbling block initially because we're all a little afraid to commit. There are so many fabulous looks out there, and many are probably represented on our social media feeds. However, this journey is about your home. And now you have a sense of what you want your home to say and offer others. This opens the door for you to identify the look and feel that will serve your priorities and your people.

You'll feel at home in surroundings that reflect your heart.

Each of us has a unique style because each of us has a unique story. Try to summarize your style in a few words. That will help you focus your efforts and make important choices. If you hire professionals, a clearly defined style will greatly improve your communication at every stage.

Style Close Up

With so many decorator terms out there, the process often starts with confusion. It helps greatly to learn the characteristics of the primary styles and see which ones match your preferences and feel beautiful to you. This should be enjoyable and helpful, never limiting. It can give you words to describe the essence of the environment you want to create. Remember that you can love a style even though you know it isn't *your* style.

One way I help my clients is by serving as a design translator. I'll look at a picture of a room with them, exploring what they like about it. Is it the light fixture? The shape of a chair? The minimalist openness? The cozy gathering of objects? I'll suggest adjectives to see what resonates with them. From this conversation, we're able to pinpoint a style or combination that helps them know what to search for as they explore design resources, gather inspiration, and build excitement.

The truth is that your unique style will likely be a combination of looks, such as modern and transitional with touches of eclectic.

Exuberance is beauty.

WILLIAM BLAKE

Pull up a chair and explore these descriptions of the nine styles I work with most frequently. These are the ones that most of my clients pursue, but there are countless others you can explore, including English country, industrial, craftsman, Hollywood, shabby chic, farmhouse, and Bohemian (which I also love).

RELAXED MODERN

This style evokes a sense of coziness and soul and captures Provençal warmth with organic wood materials, a neutral color palette, and clean lines. Relaxed modern can also embrace a mix of contrasting tones and muted pops of color. It feels completely relaxed and livable without sacrificing style or beauty. This look is foundational to what we do at Urbanology Designs.

THE NEW ART DECO

This is a slightly curvier, more polished version of relaxed modern. It is new but really gaining steam! Sculptural lines and curved geometric patterns are showcased in this look. Art deco favors burl woods with their rich, grainy patterns, high contrast materials, and a splash of glam for fun. The reinvented art deco also incorporates neutral tones in a fresh and vivacious way. This style mixes so well with relaxed modern. Find some great examples and inspiration at LuLu and Georgia's website (luluandgeorgia.com).

MODERN PARISIAN

Do you say "croissant" like a native Frenchman? And do you prefer to eat that croissant while seated on a sophisticated, velvet sofa? If so, you may be ready to embrace the charm and imperfections of this classically French-inspired look. Elaborate molding, dramatic windows, rustic marble fireplaces, worn herringbone oak floors, and vintage knickknacks are just a few whims of this effortless-meets-elegant style. White walls, chandeliers, and the use of rugs are also classic examples of this look, which is steeped in history. Today's modern Parisian vibe feels both fresh and artistic, which translates as classy and sophisticated and inviting. Take a peek at Lulu and Georgia for some modern Parisian looks.

TRADITIONAL MODERN

I like to call this modern nostalgic. It has traditional or vintage elements mixed with clean lines and modern elements. This is such a fun and bespoke style when done well. Modern meets heirloom with clean lines and vintage finds. This style is less refined than straight traditional, pulling in a cool, curated look that feels both cozy and fresh. Think white walls, a modern sofa with clean lines, an antique sideboard, and quirky vintage art. Like a good pair of jeans, you can dress this look up or down. McGee & Co. offers good examples of this look.

TRANSITIONAL MODERN

When defining your design style, is modern too sleek? Traditional too stuffy? You might like transitional modern. It's a slightly more contemporary feel than traditional modern. Less vintage flair with a mix of clean and curved lines and modern/contemporary elements. Through its simple lines, neutral color scheme, and use of light and warmth, transitional style joins the best of both the traditional and modern worlds. The furniture is classic, timeless, and clean. Color palettes are subtle with an emphasis on soft grays and whites. A lack of ornamentation and decoration with minimal accessories keeps the focus on the simplicity and sophistication. Mitchell Gold + Bob Williams is a great source for this look.

CONTEMPORARY

Contemporary interiors feature both tone-on-tone palettes as well as bold color often found in an accent wall, rug or accessories. At its foundation, contemporary style means "of the moment," so this style is ever-evolving because what is popular now will change. It feels slightly less cozy but sleeker and a bit more refined than the relaxed modern. White, taupe, and chrome are the dominating color pallets. You'll find some favorite pieces for this look at Design Within Reach, All Modern, and Crate and Barrel.

MIDCENTURY MODERN

Do you miss the look and feel of your childhood home built in the sixties? Do you gravitate to open floor plans with large, rectangular glass windows, sliding glass doors, and half walls? Are you game to buy a fiberglass chair? If so, then your design style leans toward midcentury modern. MCM broadly describes architecture, furniture, and graphic design from the middle of the twentieth century (roughly 1933 to 1965). The furniture is identified by straight, clean lines accented with smooth, curved angles. The style rarely features any fancy ornamentation or upholstery. This minimalist design commonly relies on wooden construction but can include fiberglass or metal. Colors tend to combine darker neutral tones with saturated accent colors. Check West Elm and Design Within Reach for a few key pieces.

ECLECTIC

Is your iTunes playlist filled with many genres? Does seeing matching lamps on bedside tables make you cringe? Eclectic may be calling your name. The eclectic style can be defined as a selection of what appears to be the best in various styles. It's a collection of elements gathered from different sources and put together with color, texture, shape, and finish. Eclectic allows you to express your creativity as you mix vintage and modern, elegant and casual, and whatever combinations give you joy. The challenge is to walk the thin line between contrast and chaos. When done well, eclectic shows off your style yet still adheres to the fundamentals of good design. The best way to master eclectic is to choose a few must-haves to anchor the space and then experiment with rugs, artwork, lighting, accessories, and other elements.

SCANDINAVIAN

Are you a modern minimalist who enjoys a clean, white palette? You may have some Scandinavian running through your veins. An offshoot of the midcentury modern movement, Scandinavian design introduced a popular minimalist look to the interior architecture field seen in many homes today. Scandinavian style features gentle contours, playful accent colors, and a balance of engineered and organic materials. Scandinavian furniture is simple, contemporary, and functional. A great majority of Scandinavian interiors use white with gray tones as the foundation colors. To get this clean, versatile aesthetic in your home, visit an IKEA store or make an online visit to the Danish Design Store. The ideas will be flowing!

What we love and care about will emerge in our choices when we nurture ourselves and are intentional in the design process. Our heart will show in our style, our relationships, the way we approach life, and the tiniest of details of our days. Belief in ourselves and our identities is the springboard for all our decisions in life. Let this bring you clarity and direction in your home.

WALK-THROUGH MOMENT

Write this down in your home journal or design notebook so that when you are torn between possibilities, you can return to your home base:

MY STYLE IS

AND I ALSO LIKE A LITTLE

PART II

PREPARE

FOR

BEAUTY

FOUR

CREATE WHITE SPACE AND ORDER

Sharing our evening meal as a family is a priority Eric and I established years ago. We set aside our phones and other distractions so we can be present to our five kids as we enjoy a meal prepared by one or several of us. All the kids know their way around the kitchen. And they all know to make their way around our ten-foot wood plank table come dinner time.

After we say grace, we share our high/low—a high point and a low point from the day. When friends visit the kids, they are included. Without fail, those guests will say their high point is the shared meal and conversation!

This is how we create white space in our life for what matters. This is how we carve out a physical and emotional place that is not cluttered by the stuff that can otherwise bump these priorities, such as work deadlines, online activities, or detours with just one more phone call, one more page of the book, one more minute of the video . . . one more thing.

DECLUTTER
LIKE THE
GOOD LIFE
DEPENDS
ON IT. YOU
WILL FEEL
LIGHTER AND
EXPERIENCE
MORE
CLARITY IN
EVERY FACET
OF YOUR LIFE.

In home design, intentionally creating white space is also a way to focus on what matters and to form welcoming spaces. The way to begin is by decluttering and organizing your rooms. This frees you to make design choices that nurture and delight. If you're tempted to bypass purging and organizing so you can dive into the fun of buying a new bed frame or hiring someone to paint an alcove wall, you will eventually encounter the obstacle of the stuff when the furniture or paint crew arrives. Playing musical closets with boxes of life debris is a waste of your energy. And the stuff always wins. That is, until you get intentional.

Pare Down to Build Up Purpose

My rule is, if an item is not beautiful, purposeful, and meaningful at the highest levels—then, y'all...*Give. It. Away.* In fact, before you start organizing anything, go through your home and get rid of things first. Then you bring order only to what you need and want to take up residence in your home.

I would give a single mom who has three kids and is just making ends meet the same advice I would give the married business owner with resources to put toward home renovation. Both of those women represent seasons of my own journey, and I know that focusing on home organization is one of the most powerful ways to empower oneself and invite beauty in.

By eliminating excess, we can *be* more of who we are rather than feeling burdened to add, consume, and increase belongings to define us. When you remove obstacles, you can then focus on the purpose and meaning of a space. So declutter like the good life depends on it. You will feel lighter and experience more clarity in every facet of your life. Here are two helps that will improve your mission.

Involve your spouse and the whole family. Delegate. It will lift up those around you. My older kids, Tyler, Maddie, and Lilly, are especially good about helping. When I was undergoing chemo, the house and family could not have run without their help. They saw that they mattered to our survival. You don't have to be a sick mom

Whoever is happy will
make others happy too.

ANNE FRANK

to realize you need some help—or to teach your children how valuable to the family they are.

Embrace this as a creative exercise in beautification. Organization can actually be an outlet for more of your creativity. Even if your style is eclectic and includes more objects than some other styles, you can create the white space that gives you and your family breathing room and a sense of peace.

LIVING ROOM

Surprisingly, this typically high-trafficked area can become a great place for hidden storage. The secret is in how you arrange your furniture. People think their sofas, chairs, and media cabinets need to be pushed against the walls, but there are better ways to organize a room. Pull those pieces forward a few inches or a few feet to create a proper seating space. You've just created storage space behind those pieces. Between your couch and the wall is a hidey hole for pillows, blankets, and even baskets for toys. And you've just improved your seating because it is intimate and designed for communication.

To maximize storage for linens, more toys, or even office supplies, consider placing storage bins under your couch. I developed shallow wooden drawers with rope handles. The kids can pull these drawers out when playing and slide them back under the couch when they're done—easy breezy. A rolling container made to go under beds may also work with your sofa. For a less-traditional toy box, make or get a small wooden box with no top and place toys inside little canvas sacks with drawstrings that little fingers can cinch easily.

Whether your clutter includes toys or books or technology, first eliminate what you don't need or want and then assign a place for what you keep. Some families designate the living room as a tech-free zone to increase the emotional white space. In our family, the living room is *the* tech space because our kids are not allowed to have devices upstairs. We decided years ago to preserve bedrooms for rest and peacefulness. It has been one of the best decisions we've ever made for our family.

Create White
Space and Order

KITCHEN

I bought a lovely glass milk jug that I fill from the clunky carton each week. Every time I open the fridge and see that clean silhouette and fresh milk, it makes me smile. And I always know when we are about to run out. Pretty containers and canisters can up your beauty game with ease.

Clear storage containers are my favorite choices for nearly everything in the kitchen: cereals, pastas, coffee, tea, baking ingredients, rice, oats, crackers, nuts, and more. I use glass containers with bamboo lids for many items, including raisins, nuts, and dried fruit. Large, plastic, nonbreakable containers are great for cereal. This helps my kids (especially the little ones) make good choices because the bright, illustrated boxes aren't swaying their decisions.

Baskets hold granola or protein bars, fruit snacks, applesauce packets, pretzel packs, and other favorites. Eliminating cardboard boxes from the pantry equals more space. I place age-appropriate snacks to match the height of the kids. If they can reach it, they can have it. (No fair standing on chairs!) The little ones help themselves to dried fruit on the bottom shelf, but if they want something extra special, they need to ask for permission and help.

Remove produce from its packaging as soon as you get home and store it inside glass or ceramic bowls in the fridge. Simple or ornate bowls, depending on your style, can display seasonal fruit for quick and easy access. If climate allows, display fruit on the counter to remind you to enjoy it as a treat.

Many dish cupboards have glass doors, so keeping them lean and tidy aids in ease of access and visual appeal. Pull out everything and put it on your dining table. Decide which pieces or sets matter the most to you and say goodbye to the rest. These are some of the things people commonly end up moving along: canisters that are hard to open or the wrong size, mismatched dishes that don't have functional or sentimental value, souvenir glasses and mugs, and those pesky plastic food containers with missing lids. (The lids are probably hanging out with missing socks somewhere in the universe.)

DINING ROOM

I'll keep this simple: At all costs, avoid the temptation to set stuff on your table. Otherwise, the day will come when you want to host a gathering and entertain your friends, but one look at that dining table leaves you reconsidering and likely canceling. Sorting through weeks and weeks of clutter and junk mail is overwhelming. At these moments, the prospect of inviting someone into your home feels exhausting and embarrassing. But implementing systems and rules, like "no junk on the table," makes a quick cleanup easy. And all that resentment and shame at the state of your home? *Poof!* Gone with the piles.

SMALL COAT CLOSETS

Consider eliminating the rod and hangers from your coat closet. Look at the small area with possibility and creativity. Add a row of hooks or use an over-the-door rack with five hooks for raincoats or jackets that have hoods. Below these jackets, right in line with the interior doorknob, forego traditional hooks and permanently attach a row of three hardware clips, similar to those found on a clipboard. These make it so easy to hang and display any kind of lightweight jacket or sweater.

Hang a row or two of low shelves for shoes. A couple feet above those, hang two to eight pegs for your kids to hang backpacks. Two more shelves, spaced a little wider apart from each other, can house wicker baskets for scarves, gloves, mittens, ball caps, umbrellas, pet supplies, or those miscellaneous items you might need just as you're running out the door.

BEDROOMS

Your bedroom is your most intimate space, yet it's the easiest to neglect. If the living room is nice, the kitchen is clean, the children are fed, and so on, who cares if our bedroom is shipshape, right? But honey, your bedroom is your sanctuary, and taking care of it is the first step in taking care of yourself.

Give yourself a gift each evening by making your bed each morning. Simple actions will inspire you to care for your space with more consistency. If you elevate how you think about your room, you'll protect the ways it provides you a haven for recovering and refueling. What could be more important?

You and your spouse might need to compromise in your bedroom space to be sure each person has elements of storage, organization, and comfort. Your husband might like a row of bins for books and technology and socks while you prefer a dresser in your style that houses your items. Other options include side tables, chests, armoires, storage ottomans, and tall baskets. Which ones speak to you and your style? Choices that bring function and beauty to your sanctuary will bring rest to your spirit.

———

The beauty of open space and order has emerged. You've done the good work (and grunt work) so you'll be ready to make design and decor decisions unhindered by stuff. Remember, each step leads to the next as we walk through this experience and your home. When everything is in its place, you can envision the big picture. Does everything need to change? Or just some of it? Now that you've pared down and organized, identify what you need so you can transform your house into a home that reflects who you are and brings you joy and inspiration every single day.

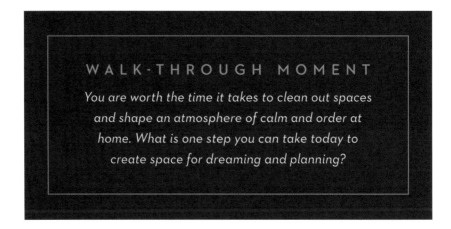

FIVE

WELCOME CHALLENGES AS OPPORTUNITIES

D uring a recent walk-through session, a client and I stood looking at her over-crowded living room. It wasn't full of partygoers; it was brimming with furniture representing one or two styles too many to pass as eclectic. Disaster? Not by a long shot. Opportunity? Definitely. We moved on through the house. Her long, narrow family room had her grandmother's game table, a large console with technology cords sprawling, a large couch, workout equipment, and a medium-sized rug dwarfed by the room measurements. They use the room a lot, so it serves the family well, but it feels random, and she longs for a casual but cozy intentionality.

She motions to the old game table. "Friends keep telling me to get rid of these chairs or recover them, but I have such happy childhood memories around this table . . . " Her voice trails off, and I get it. I see what this space can be . . . and it will include that table and those chairs.

Each of these challenges becomes an opportunity to get creative and to personalize a space so it feels true to the people who live there. When you run into challenges, you'll be able to move toward solutions once you present yourself with this dialogue:

"Is it a disaster?" No.

"Is it an opportunity?" Yes.

I've seen all kinds of strange layouts, congested rooms, awkward windows, and quirky slopes or angles. Sometimes I hit a brick wall—and that's not a metaphor, but an actual challenge! I enjoy walking into a problem zone in a home and envisioning what could help, improve, or transform that area into a space that is useful and loved.

In the example I just gave, my suggestions were simple. The furniture-stuffed living room simply required prioritizing, pruning, and rearranging. Two rustic chairs could be moved to the family cabin, leaving an eclectic but complementary mix of two styles in the living room. I suggested they create a conversation area with two of the chairs positioned so they work with the whole and are angled to also enjoy the view of the backyard through a beautiful, large window.

As for the family room, my list was more extensive but still simple. Anchor the rambling room with an extra-large rug, complement the retro game table with a cupboard of classic boardgames, and transform the unused area behind the couch into a shuffleboard setup (I told you it was a long room!). Place large art on the big wall—such as a charming scoreboard or the family name in large letters—instead of filling it with kitschy game-room posters and small signs. Hire a tech pro or electrician to reduce the number of cables, or move the expansive entertainment center slightly to hide the modem and cords and leave room to access them.

Sometimes it takes only a few actions to transform a random room into a cohesive, welcoming space for an active family.

Different Obstacles, Same Lesson

Sometimes challenges are not related to the space but are tied to finances, time, and what homeowners are able to do on their own. Success comes to those who are willing to face challenges, fears, and risks and seek creative or practical solutions. I live for that moment when I see the possibility first instead of the problem. You will too.

———

My girls, Maddison and Lillian, were twelve and eleven when it was time for me to improve on their small, bleak, shared room. They slept in dark bunkbeds, and their belongings migrated around the dismal space without a permanent spot to call home. I knew our active, creative girls were going to struggle with the space because it was a poorly arranged room—more like a barracks than a sanctuary.

I started exactly as I started our journey in this book: I began to dream. I entered the room with a notepad and walked around the perimeter. I sat cross-legged on the floor in every corner and then in the middle. I measured each nook.

Soon the dream emerged.

I envisioned a Scandia-Bohemian look. Airy and pretty with intentional elements of function and flair to suit my girls. This room lacked horizontal space but was stellar with vertical space. "Lofty, flowy, unique . . ." these words suited the potential. With the hope of a style and vision, I was ready to acknowledge the challenges. I confess my heart races a bit with excitement when I enter this phase. This was a puzzle I couldn't wait to figure out because it would bless my girls greatly.

I identified one big-picture challenge and three main decor challenges so I could avoid following every rabbit trail of possibility. Too many options can make us freeze up, just as a big challenge can.

I LIVE FOR THAT MOMENT WHEN I SEE THE POSSIBILITY FIRST INSTEAD OF THE PROBLEM. YOU WILL TOO.

BIG·PICTURE CHALLENGE: Budget

We couldn't spend much. Eric and I set a budget. Each purchase had to be valuable to the vision. I mentioned that I get giddy when presented with a challenge, right?

CHALLENGE: Dark and Small

Solutions:

— Replaced the heavy window blinds with a light and airy curtain—embellished with fringe, of course.

— Added a few can lights and a stunning beaded chandelier that gets rave reviews from the girls' friends and from our online community.

— Paint! We chose a white for the twelve-foot ceilings and upper part of the walls and then a soft, amazing blush color for the main walls. (It happens to be called Blush, by Benjamin Moore.)

CHALLENGE: Terrible, Matted-Down Carpet

Solutions:

— Ripped out the carpet and laid five-inch natural maple boards for a Boho-chic vibe.

— Selected a few throw rugs to add warmth for cold days and barefooted teens heading for bed.

CHALLENGE: Storage and Functional Furniture for a Small Space

Solutions:

— Built a custom high bunk bed with storage to make the most of vertical space. This involved constructing a support wall to hold the beds and then building a ladder into the wall for bunk access. That ladder saved so much precious space.

— Designed the lower third of the bed structure with storage cubbies.

— Preserved a small area under the cubbies to house a mattress for sleepovers.

- Replaced the closet door with a macramé curtain. This saved room and embraced the style.

- Installed a narrow, floating wall desk with a peg board system for customized shelving and storage.

- Placed a convenient bookshelf on the way to the top bunk for quick access.

- Unique touches: The momentum to keep adding functional and pretty elements led to a reading nook made from a stack of cushions and a canopy.

The blush and gold chair on wheels could not be better. The unique feather mobile floating above the desk is handmade by the Dream Barn. The personalized calligraphy banner made by Jessica Shubert of Scripted Love Calligraphy hangs above the bathroom door.

Facing Challenges with Faith . . . and Help

When our youngest daughter, Avery, was diagnosed with leukemia at the fragile age of five months, we were at our most vulnerable. We had to be wise, proactive, prayerful, and vested in each decision.

We were thrown into a new world of doctors, procedures, and protocols to protect Avery and her weakened immune system. The team at Cook Children's Medical Center in Fort Worth saw our wide eyes and trembling hands, and they carefully explained what needed to happen. Avery had to stay in the hospital 24/7 during and between treatments. It was excruciating to not have her home, but we knew this plan was vital to her survival.

A trauma of this magnitude presents unexpected struggles, and it reveals what it takes to face all challenges: You need help even when you aren't sure what to ask for.

While our tired minds struggled with logistics, my sister Cindy, a nurse, called and said she was quitting her job and moving to be near us. I wept at such generosity. She fulfilled that promise to help care for our kids at home (as she cared for her own family) and to make sure we had what we needed to remain strong for Avery.

Seven months later we brought Avery home. Now, years later, she remains cancer-free. Her cancer journey happened before mine, so my baby daughter was my example of endurance and hope when my labs revealed a challenging path. I learned to ask for help and receive it on behalf of Avery and later for myself and our family.

I came out the other side of this trial with a greater sensitivity and desire to help others. Serving is a joy. And helping a family create a sanctuary is a privilege I won't ever take lightly. You never know the ways a home will nurture people in their lifetime.

The Helpers

My personal challenges and my professional experiences have given me a big heart for the client who is figuring out how to ask for help. If you know you need help to let beauty emerge, but you aren't sure what kind, you're not alone. My encouragement: Don't let it be the stall point in your journey.

When I do an initial consult with a prospective client, I empower them with clarification about who does what professionally. My clients entrust their sanctuary to me. The results matter. The money they are investing matters. The impact the choices will have on the family matters. Instead of pushing forward in uncertainty, determine who will help you most.

INTERIOR DESIGNER

This person works with a client to create spaces that are attractive, safe, and functional. They might help with cabinet selection, paint colors, and even the final accessory placement. If you're hiring an architect and a designer, which is very common, involve the designer when the plans have been drawn up but before they have been finalized so they can look for opportunities that may have been missed.

ARCHITECT

Start here if you are moving many walls or adding on to an existing structure. The architect assesses and calculates the math behind your vision and can help you determine whether what you want will fit and be up to code. After taking measurements, they can draw up plans to represent the safe and proper way to implement the structural changes you want.

STRUCTURAL ENGINEER

Sometimes you can skip the architect and hire a structural engineer to verify whether you can knock down an existing wall without adding more support.

GENERAL CONTRACTOR

A general contractor oversees the entire project and is valuable if you lack wisdom in home building or can't be on-site daily. The

Never lose an opportunity of seeing anything beautiful, for beauty is God's handwriting.

RALPH WALDO EMERSON

temptation can be to save and DIY, but I've seen clients try this and then spend more money to do it right the second time around.

ELECTRICIAN AND PLUMBER

For big projects and for day-to-day improvements or concerns in a home, these are the most-called professionals. Seek their help rather than do the work yourself.

CARPENTER

Carpenters can customize your home by adding crown molding, shelving, or the perfect staircase (sometimes with help from metal-workers). They handle anything made from wood or drywall. A cabinetmaker specializes in making pieces with drawers and sliding mechanisms and helps integrate appliances with cabinetry.

PAINTER

Some painters specialize in interior or exterior painting; others do both. Get multiple bids and choose someone who will care about the details that matter to you. Always note if the bid includes the price and quality of the paint they will be using.

SPECIALISTS

A window-treatment specialist comes after your windows and trim have been installed. They take measurements and help you pick out shutters, blinds, shades, and curtains. Most companies have suppliers and installers. An audio-visual specialist doesn't come to help you find your remote (too bad, right?), but they can set up your home to function from your smart phone or add surround sound in a media room. They might even eliminate the remote altogether!

How to Hire Professionals

Once you determine the kind of professional you need for the project, start researching. Ask for recommendations from people you trust. And check sources like Houzz for reviews and to see who does projects like yours.

Our firm works with teams we have vetted. There is no reason you can't do the same! Most contractors and subcontractors will not charge for an initial consultation. Collect several bids. Compare not only the cost but also work quality, reputation, communication skills, and so on.

Choose a professional who will listen to you and make your priorities their own. Be as detailed as possible about your vision, and use reference photos. Speaking up for what matters to you will serve your home well.

Questions and research won't delay your dream. When you have identified your challenges and clarified a stirring vision of what you want to focus on, your "someday" dream is ready for the foundation to be laid. The excitement keeps building!

WALK-THROUGH MOMENT

Ask, "What could this room become? How could this space bless someone?" Identify your big-picture challenges and secondary ones. Now, what help do you need to see beauty emerge in your home?

SIX

TRUST THE PROMISE OF A PLAN

Design shows that air 24/7 have delighted us and spoiled us. In less than an hour, we see a whole room—or house!—renovated and redesigned. In real life, we have no montage magic. The transformation requires a plan and step-by-step actions. Oh, and a wee bit of patience.

A plan allows you to meet the predicted challenges as well as the unanticipated ones. Three years after I founded Urbanology Designs, I was ready to move our office out of our home and into a space we could claim for our own. And this gave me a new space to design!

I had my heart set on buying a local fire station that had been abandoned for years. It's located near my church, and every time I drove by, I stared at it with excitement. I didn't see the run-down building that other passersby did; I saw the beautiful creation it would become, complete with an attractive event space, meeting rooms, and private office suites to rent.

PATIENCE,

MODIFICATION,

AND

ASSESSMENT

ARE REQUIRED

FOR ANY

WORTHWHILE

PROCESS.

I saw huge windows along the front and a wide staircase leading to a modern, cozy loft for our main office. It would represent the company's relaxed, nostalgic modern style with plenty of unique touches. Let me tell you, I was so inspired when I saw all the possibilities.

I did the research, made plans, did more research...and I bought the building! We were on our way to the vision.

Then complications came.

I had to fire our original contractor. We lost time and money. I was so frustrated. Clients pay me to oversee the schedule of their projects, so why wasn't I able to keep my own on track? It was a reminder that God's timing is perfect. In the additional fifteen months it took to create the dream, we not only met the right contractor but also came up with the money we needed to make this space everything it could be.

What helped? The plan. There were unfortunate happenings and glitches. But each time, I could return to my plan and my non-negotiable objectives and hold fast. The promise of a plan is not that everything goes perfectly, but that everything can continue in the direction of your goal. Patience, modification, and assessment are required for any worthwhile process.

When Waiting Is Part of the Plan

When I'm facing an issue that feels bigger than anything I've dealt with before, Eric reminds me of all I've walked through. "Ginger, remember how that one challenge bowled you over a couple years ago? Now it would be a blip on your radar." So true! I have grown from each challenge. Remember...God *will* use all things, including delays or detours.

At age twenty-one, I married a man who was charming and strong. But after saying our vows, he was unkind, demeaning, and unfaithful. My hope for a loving partnership went up in flames. Out of those ashes, I became a single mom of two children. Shortly after my husband and I separated but before the divorce finalized, I adopted

my nephew Tyler. My sister Laura had tragically passed away, and I knew Tyler was meant to be a part of my immediate family.

I leaned into God's strength more than ever before. I regained lost confidence in my beauty and worth as God made me. Though I had the desire for a godly life partner, I told the Lord that he came before my hope for a husband.

Because I did that, my heart and life were prepared when I met Eric during my church's disaster-relief mission on the south coast of Texas. He was called away suddenly when his father passed away from a heart attack. Before he left, he asked if I'd bring his belongings home to Fort Worth. Later, when he came to my house to collect his things, we talked about grief, hope, and faith. I was drawn to his commitment to God. And during next visits, I shared about my childhood and first marriage. That's when I saw something I'd never seen before: Eric was angry and hurt on my behalf. His protective kindness made me feel safe.

In time, it was clear we were interested in one another, but we wanted to wait on God's timing. We agreed that while Eric went camping, we would both pray about us. When he returned, we sat down on my porch and shared what we'd both heard during prayer: *Not yet.*

Waiting is difficult in matters of the heart. However, today I am grateful because the Lord taught me how to view waiting on him—not as a departure from plans, but as part of his best plan. Later, when Eric and I knew God was leading us to be married, our commitment was all the sweeter. We didn't want shortcuts; we wanted to do things right so that we honored God and our family. Through our waiting, praying, and partnering, Eric was the one who reinforced the beauty of God's plan even though we couldn't see what was up ahead. And when we faced the urge to trust human plans because they were more convenient, his patience helped me understand that we were investing our hope and love in a bigger picture that would unfold for years to come.

Learning that lesson of trusting and waiting in my personal life helped me stay anchored and sane during the delays building the Urban Firehouse. When I wanted to cry, Eric pointed out the blessings and reminded me of God's faithfulness. If everything had gone according to my plan, I would have missed working with the right contractors, who were true partners and supported my creativity and goals at every stage. The delay we experienced allowed us to generate more revenue and bring on board amazing collaborators who saw the vision of what we were doing and wanted to be a part of it: Farrow & Ball, Room and Board, Monogram, Zia Tile, Burlington Design Gallery, and local artisans. These collaborations elevated the space beyond what I could have imagined.

This might be what you need to hear today...blessings come in the waiting. And in my situation, the result was better than the dream. On opening day, I was deeply grateful that my plans had not unfolded perfectly, but God's plan had.

Nurture your dream and the vision. Create a plan. And trust the next step. A plan based on your heart purpose and fulfilled with patience helps you notice solutions and ideas. It empowers you to respond to surprises with hope rather than defeat. And when things don't go your way, look at how the changes might serve a greater purpose. The promise of any plan is that any detours and mistakes become our teachers in patience, wisdom, experience, and faith.

Your Boardroom

The wonderful array of online resources are like power tools for planning. You can create a design board to visualize and express your style, preferences, and function needs. All of these can come together in a gallery of images of furniture, colors, room shapes and sizes, appliances, lighting, accessories...the list goes on.

Those who are creative love all the options. Those who don't see themselves as creative love the world of images and offerings available that can transform a vague idea of a "white couch" to a very specific style and size for what will best serve them. Even clients who don't often use digital resources soon fall in love with this particular way of using technology to shift their dream from ideas to images.

Watching a design board of your room come together is exciting and empowering. This will keep you on track for all that follows. I recommend that you start a Pinterest board or a Houzz idea book. On Houzz, you can source products, read helpful blogs, find interior designers and builders, and save and organize photos in an idea book. It's one of the most organized and user-friendly platforms out there. It's a great tool for both the consumer and designer. I encourage my clients to use it, especially in the beginning stages of identifying a vision and style preferences.

Start with a fresh board when you get serious about your project. Material you've gathered over the years won't necessarily reflect your current goals. Get picky. Save only the images of rooms and ideas that make your heart leap! The "okays" don't need to land

There is nothing that
makes its way more directly
to the soul than beauty.

JOSEPH ADDISON

here. It's also helpful if your spouse has their own board. Two things can happen: Either you will see patterns emerge of things you both gravitate toward, or you will confirm your suspicion that you are opposites. Wherever you land, there is hope. When tastes and styles differ, look at which elements from each person's style you can blend in a way that is beautiful and intentional.

What to Expect When You're Expecting Change and Beauty

I'm a mom and a designer. I can tell you without a doubt that the emotional journey through the design process is very similar to the cycle of emotions a couple experiences as they await the arrival of their baby. And if you really want a memorable rollercoaster, try tackling design projects while pregnant. Been there. Done that.

Initial emotions for the baby scenario go something like this: "We're going to have a baby!" said with excitement and wonder. These emotions will flip-flop a few times with anxiety and uncertainty: "Oh, my goodness…we're having a baby," said with anxiety. "How do we prepare? Our to-do list just quadrupled. We need to clean out that office-turned-den-turned-storage room immediately. Our home will never be the same. Are we ready for this? We need help!"

If you replace the word "baby" with "remodel," that's pretty spot-on for the flow between joy and uncertainty during the stages of a larger home or room redesign. To assure you that what you're feeling is completely normal, I'll share the emotional journey we have identified when working with clients and have experienced personally. Whether you are doing this on your own or you've hired someone like me, here is what you can expect.

1 DREAM AND BELIEVE.

The fun begins as you imagine what could be.

EMOTIONS AND THOUGHTS:
Energy. Awakening. Hesitation. Conviction. *Could I? What is my dream? I am worthy of beauty.*

2 IDENTIFY CHALLENGES AND POSSIBILITIES.

This is the "I'm doing this!" moment in the personal journey.

EMOTIONS AND THOUGHTS:
Anticipation! Butterfly feelings of possibility. *There is hope for a change. Those seemingly huge what-ifs are manageable.*

3 PRIORITIZE AND COMMIT.

Determine what matters most and move forward. If you are working with a professional, identify the terms of service.

EMOTIONS AND THOUGHTS:
Anxiety lightens. Relief. *I understand the process. This makes sense. It is doable.*

4 RESEARCH AND EXPLORE.

This is your homework stage whether you are working independently or with a professional. At this stage, I provide clients with a list of questions to be sure I understand their wants and needs and challenges.

EMOTIONS AND THOUGHTS:
Joy. Curiosity. Some overwhelm by the abundance of choices. *I better understand what I want. There are a lot of decisions to make. I hope I don't get lost.*

5 MAKE A PLAN.

Identify challenges and when and where you'll want professional input or help. If you hire a designer, this stage includes the site survey, design development, and design board presentation.

EMOTIONS AND THOUGHTS:
Slight overwhelm followed by security. Nervous excitement. *What was I thinking? Waiting is hard. My overwhelm is dissolving into hope with each step forward.*

6 HUNT AND GATHER.

This is the time to "measure twice, buy once." In the professional cycle, this includes final approval and implementation of plans.

EMOTIONS AND THOUGHTS:
Empowerment. Confidence. *This is really happening! I can see the vision unfolding. The momentum is exhilarating.*

7 DESIGN THE BEAUTY.

Schedule professionals helping with tiling, painting, plumbing, and so on. Receive purchases, put things in place, adjust big and small details on your personal journey. When working with a professional, this is the last stage of collaboration and installation.

EMOTIONS AND THOUGHTS:
Satisfaction. Joy. Pride. Awe. *The puzzle pieces have come together, and I'm blown away by the final result. I'm grateful for every part of the process because now I get to live in the beauty I had only dreamed of.*

You are empowered with your priorities, your heart's desire, your initial plan, and an awareness of what to expect in the journey going forward—including the result of beauty and delight in your home. So are you ready to say yes to the adventure?

WALK-THROUGH MOMENT

When have you waited for something good to unfold? Look around your home and soak in the hope of an emerging beauty. To inspire the journey, write down the first three steps of your plan and post it where you will see it daily.

This is a dive-in exploration and summary. Are you ready? Previous chapters have prepared us for the planning phase and this *home-work* (which is so much more fun than algebra, I promise). Simply put, this will recap and refine your vision and priorities.

—What is your dream?

—What are your plumb line and mission statement for your home?

—What style or style combo have you identified as your own?

—What mood/feeling do you want the space to have for daily living?

—What is your big-picture challenge for the room you'll redesign first?

—Will you ask professionals to help you with any stages of the process? If you are hiring, which category of professional suits your needs?

—Now that you've done some research, what is your next step in communicating with the professional?

— Who is involved in the final decisions? Are you making the choices or partnering with a spouse? Are you redesigning a kid's bedroom and asking what they like? This is important to determine even if you are working with a professional.

— What is nonnegotiable?

— What is your timeline?

— On a scale of one to five, five being the fastest, how quickly do you make decisions? (Some advice: If you are slow to make decisions, partner with someone who can make quick decisions.)

— What colors do you love? Which ones don't you like?

— What are some things you already love about this space?

— What pieces of furniture in your home do you love or not love?

— What inspired you to move forward to make a change?

PART III

IMMERSE
IN
BEAUTY

SEVEN

LAY THE GROUNDWORK

WOOD AND ALTERNATIVE FLOORING

Our homes can become sanctuaries when we tend to them with a big-picture perspective. Take it all in. Consider whether the mood you desire is reflected when you look up, down, and around. A home that immerses people in beauty will inspire and nurture their spirits. Have you ever entered a living room and immediately felt welcomed? Have you been drawn to the image of a bedroom online and you aren't sure why, but it invites you to take a deep breath? Those feelings arise when a space works as a whole. My friend, this can be the experience in your home too.

So many experiences in my life have shown me that it's easy to get tossed by the wind if we're not planted firmly. In the early steps toward a new venture or when adjusting to life after a big change, our footing can be unsure. If we start from the groundwork of love, family, and faith, we can move into our lives with courage and assurance. Let's determine our priorities and plan our life and home choices around what matters most.

Establish a beautiful home by first focusing on what supports you—your flooring foundation. Choosing what you love will ground your home and elevate it with style, grace, and enduring beauty.

Foundation Fundamentals

The most-used element of the home is often the most ignored. What are you standing on right now? Do you like it? Does it add beauty and ambience to your space? When was the last time you gave your floors some attention?

In design projects, I refer to the floor as the fifth wall—the other four couldn't stand without the fifth to hold them up. This foundation is one of the most important elements to consider. You want your flooring choices to support the way you live, and you want the color, texture, and pattern of the flooring to serve all your other choices, including wall color and furniture.

WOOD FLOORING

Always my first choice! And my first recommendation for authentic, timeless flooring is white oak. It is durable, practical, impervious to the elements, faithful to the end. Wood flooring adds warmth, character, and value to a home. There are also many creative floor patterns that can be done with a wood plank. Herringbone, double herringbone, parquet, chevron, staggered, brick bond, stack bond, wood strip, and mosaic are just a few of the options. You can also achieve a specific look with the width of the board you choose.

Hardwood. Wood flooring is a great long-term investment because it can be sanded and restained in practically any color. It is far more versatile than most people think. When sanding down a worn floor or outdated color, I always suggest resealing it with a matte sealer instead of a glossy finish. A high sheen shows every imperfection

and can sometimes feel manufactured. A matte finish creates a luxurious and handmade feel.

Engineered. This is similar to hardwood in that it is real wood, but it has been layered with a backing to make it more durable and easier to install.

Oil-rubbed. This type of wood floor is gaining popularity because it uses fewer chemicals in the sealing process. You can also spot-repair scrapes or damages instead of sanding down the entire floor. The downside is it takes more yearly maintenance and isn't as strong against damage.

I finally had the chance to install my dream floor at the Urban Fire-house. It was a beautiful, wide, white-oak plank. I had been recommending this to my clients for years, and now it was finally my turn. It was something I had to wait for. I couldn't justify tearing out the beautiful dark hickory hardwood in my own home, so when the day came for me to install floors in my "second home," I was thrilled. I knew the impact these floors would make. Light in color but still warm and inviting. What a great foundation for any room, home, or office. They are durable and easy to clean, and they don't show every speck of dirt.

OTHER FLOORING OPTIONS

Laminate. This is a mostly wood product but is sealed with plastics for durability. It can lack the depth and character of real wood, so be sure to look at samples in different lighting.

Luxury vinyl flooring. One of the newest flooring options, this takes the durability and composition of vinyl and combines them in the plank form of laminate to make a more realistic-looking vinyl that's tougher than laminate. Families commonly request vinyl flooring when they have large dogs and are worried about their floor getting scratched. A good quality vinyl will hold up against

CHOOSING WHAT YOU LOVE WILL GROUND YOUR HOME AND ELEVATE IT WITH STYLE, GRACE, AND ENDURING BEAUTY.

this type of wear and tear. The top layer is also water resistant, making it a practical choice for areas more likely to get wet.

Ceramic tile. Durable, classic, and versatile clay tiles come in a large array of shapes, styles, and colors and can work just about anywhere. Mosaics can be exotic and gorgeous. If you're looking to save money, go with polished ceramic tiles in classic shapes, like subway or hexagon. These are excellent and affordable options for either flooring or backsplashes.

When there's room in the budget to splurge, tile can become a beautiful focal point. We love marble tiles in bathrooms or kitchens, handmade porcelain or terra-cotta tiles in classic shapes, and even painted cement. With all kinds of tile, we typically choose grout as close as possible in color to the tile itself for a seamless look.

Porcelain tile. This is less porous than other tile, so it's great for wet areas. It's more costly than ceramic though.

Natural stone. Marble, travertine, slate, and quartzite are among the many natural stone options. These are generally porous and require more maintenance but add natural beauty to your spaces.

Concrete. Poured straight onto the floor, smoothed out, and left to dry, this is one of the most economical flooring options and can be beautiful in a modern home or office. It is hard underfoot, which makes it less desirable to some. If rugs are used really well, this is another one of my favorite looks.

Carpet. The softest option and a preference for many in colder climes. There are a variety of piles, so enjoy exploring options instead of going for the tan, builder-grade material. The best of both worlds might be to pair hardwood or tile floors with well-placed rugs. We'll explore rugs (oh, how I love them!) in chapter 11 so you can see how to arrange them with your favorite furniture pieces in your beloved spaces.

Floored by All the Choices

If the many options are adding stress, step back for a moment and choose a few factors that matter most for you. Looking at floors from a new angle will help you narrow down the list.

COLOR AND TONES

Consider the color of your furniture. I recommend having some visual separation between the floor and your furnishings. A rug can often do the trick, but so can contrasting furniture. I like to look at the undertones in my wood floor and use either the lighter or darker color to help me make a complementary furniture selection. A subtle contrast adds interest and value.

Light colors create a sunnier, happier feel and help small spaces. Dark colors serve larger, dramatic spaces. Gray is peaceful; browns are rustic and natural. The darker shades will show more dirt and scratches. Floor color options, like paint colors, take on different tones in varying degrees of light. Look at samples at different times during the day and under varied artificial light.

MAINTENANCE REQUIREMENTS

Be maintenance minded when making choices. Stone tiles need to be polished and sealed every few years, natural hardwood needs to be refinished at least once a decade, tiles need deep scrubbing to clean the grout, and carpet needs frequent steam cleaning and vacuuming.

STORY HEIGHT

Some flooring types are not appropriate for below-grade or higher floors of a home or building. Suspended floors tend to flex as they age and can cause cracks in slabs of stone. Basements are not well-suited to hardwood and carpet because of the potential for moisture and flooding.

Where we love is home—
home that our feet may
leave, but not our hearts.

OLIVER WENDELL
HOLMES SR.

INSTALLATION EASE

Custom flooring will take longer to order and install, while some sheet vinyl, carpet, and locking laminate flooring can be installed quickly.

OVERALL DURABILITY AND FUTURE CHALLENGES

Consider your needs and the daily usage of each room. I'm often asked if wood flooring can be used in kitchens. Yes! If you spill, just make sure to wipe it up quickly. Your floors will not only last in this high-traffic area but also develop a rich patina over time. And as we mentioned, you are always able to sand and restain when the time comes. Hardwood species vary in durability, grain patterns, and color. Oak, maple, and hickory are among the most common choices due to their hardness. Exotic woods like mahogany and Brazilian cherry aren't as durable but are prized for their striking appearance. Pine can be a more affordable option but is more susceptible to scratches because it is softer. Kitchens, like bathrooms and entryways, need a durable selection to make life easier.

Multiple Flooring Styles

You may choose to include various flooring styles in your home. The standard way to transition from one to the other is to install transition strips. Flooring styles don't have to be the same or even the same color, but they should complement each other.

More than two materials per floor will cause your space to feel cluttered. Bathrooms and laundry rooms are the exception. It can be fun and totally appropriate to change it up in these spaces. When transitioning from one flooring type to another where the transition is evident, make sure the materials are not too similar. If you're trying to present them visually as the same, it will feel off and disjointed. The goal is not to match but to coordinate, to choose materials that go well together. For example, if you transition from tile to hardwood or from hardwood to carpet, look for undertones that complement each other.

Friend, take it all in with 360 degrees of gratitude. The histories that have created the metaphorical ground beneath us are worthy and lovely. Let's be proud of the foundation of experiences we can claim. Let's be thankful for where we stand, what we stand upon, and the beauty that envelops us. This perspective will help us make decisions from the heart.

I for one am thankful that your authenticity and unique story create a welcoming refuge of beauty. This is what the world needs.

WALK-THROUGH MOMENT

Pay attention to what you are standing on. What changes or improvements in flooring do you think will support your overall vision?

EIGHT

LET IN THE LIGHT

WINDOWS AND LIGHTING

The very first thing I do when I walk into a client's home is ask, "May I turn on every light and open every curtain?"

We all have access to one of the most transforming design elements, and yet I'm always stunned that so many people miss out on immersing themselves and their sanctuary in light. Natural light has many benefits, including providing vitamin D, enhancing sleep cycles, improving mood, and increasing productivity. Illumination from well-placed fixtures also has great rewards for our lifestyles and mindsets.

A combination of light from nature and from selected ambient, task, and accent lighting will open your space for greater joy, purpose, function, and beauty. The room that's brightened just right welcomes everyone who enters and increases the possibility for you to use the space exactly how you intended.

The Wonder of Windows

They say eyes are the windows to the soul. So, what are windows? In my opinion, windows are portals of beauty and illumination in a home. They let natural light into the home—the best mood lifter and design secret there is. In my opinion, the well-lit home is nothing short of magical. My first priority is to always maximize and highlight natural lighting.

The frame of a window and the covering treatment create a functional art piece on a wall. And even if a window doesn't overlook a breathtaking landscape, it provides a visual connection to the environment and community. If you have an eyesore view, your treatment choice will elevate the window's aesthetic value and turn an obstacle into an opportunity. Beauty will emerge in the filtered light cascading through fabric in tones that support your style, whether that is cheery or dramatic, neutral or colorful, casual or elegant.

I live in Texas where many folks keep the blinds drawn or have heavy curtains to block the heat. If you deal with high temperatures, consider installing windows that block UV rays or adding UV film to current ones. If privacy is an issue, let your landscape be a part of your solution! Plant privacy shrubs or trees or add a privacy fence for some coverage from the street or sidewalk. It's so important not to miss out on the gift of light.

Treat Your Windows Right

Pleasing window treatments aren't merely finishing touches but are a significant foundational element for a well-designed space. The best tip in window coverings is to hang high and wide. This gives the illusion of bigger windows. Hang the rod at least one-half to two-thirds of the distance between the window and the ceiling. If the ceilings are vaulted, hang the rod about one foot above the window. Extend the rod ten to twelve inches on either side of the window.

WINDOWS ARE PORTALS OF BEAUTY AND ILLUMINATION IN A HOME.

PANELS

Drapery panels instantly make a space more polished and elevated. They lead the eye upward and soften a room. I often recommend neutral hues such as white, ecru, or soft gray. A linen-blend fabric will gather and drape well whether open or closed. I prefer drapery rings for hardware and mounting. Here are a few tips:

— There are endless options for linings and hardware. The fuller the look of the panels, the better. To add fullness, we like to use panels that are one and a half to two times the width of the window.

— Have the curtains just kiss the floor unless you are going for a puddled look. If they hang above the floors more than a half an inch, they can look awkward.

— For depth of texture, layer with curtain panels and window shades.

———

Window treatments can introduce lush texture and dimension into the space. Ashley Robertson, a fashion and lifestyle expert and writer, invited us to design her home. Her master bedroom provides a great example of a robust window treatment (see page 198). These panels are double width, meaning two standard-width panels are sewn together.

This living room remodel in a town not far from our Urbanology Designs' home base offers a breathtaking example of height and drama.

PLEAT STYLES

Whether you are having curtains made or looking for options at retail outlets, there are pleat possibilities to complement the look you want. My favorites are the ripple fold, Parisian pleat, pinch pleat with the double fold, and French pleat.

Ripple fold: pleating is achieved through the spacing of the carriers

Rod pocket: a sewn casing around the rod

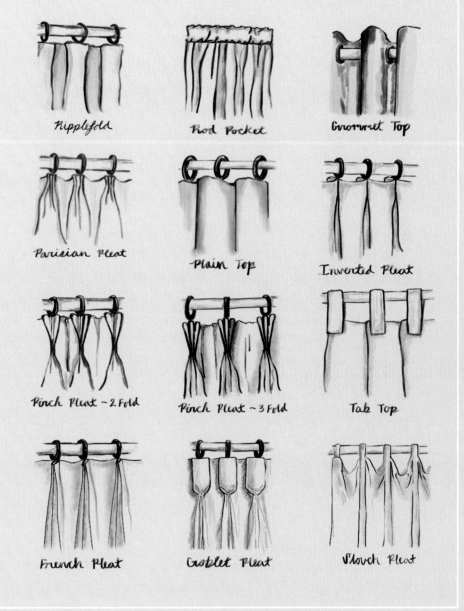

Ripplefold

Rod Pocket

Grommet Top

Parisian Pleat

Plain Top

Inverted Pleat

Pinch Pleat ~ 2 Fold

Pinch Pleat ~ 3 Fold

Tab Top

French Pleat

Goblet Pleat

Slouch Pleat

Grommet top: round, metal openings at the curtain tops

Parisian pleat: fabric is collected at the top of the flute

Plain top: fabric loosely flows from the track

Inverted pleat: fullness of drape is controlled on the back side of fabric

Pinch pleat: double fold at top of fabric

Pinch pleat: triple fold at top of fabric

Tab top: fabric loops around the rod

French pleat: controlled fullness with a sleek header

Goblet pleat: wine-glass shaped formed by pleat

Slouch pleat: large, relaxed pleats

SHADES

People are astonished at the many styles of shades that are available. They are versatile and functional and don't lose one bit of beauty.

—For a modern, no-fuss look, I recommend roller shades. They blend seamlessly into the mounting of the window and still offer functionality.

—For spaces that call for a touch of elegance, a Roman shade in a neutral, linen-blend fabric is divine. Roman shades are fabric window coverings that stack neatly at the top of the window when retracted. Some retail stores carry ready-made sizes, but these often need to be custom made in order to properly fit your window and give that beautifully tailored look.

Some pleat options are modern; others are more complex and formal. My two favorite styles for Roman shades are the flat fold and the relaxed pleat, which droops slightly at the bottom, forming a smile.

SHADE STYLES

Flat fold: a singular piece of fabric containing no seams

Soft fold: continuous loops of fabric through the entire shade

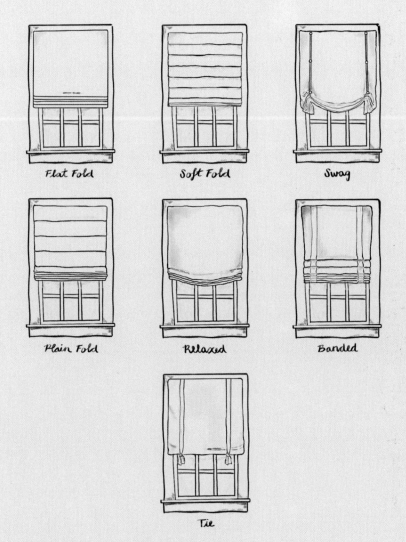

Flat Fold

Soft Fold

Swag

Plain Fold

Relaxed

Banded

Tie

The best and most beautiful
things in the world cannot be
seen or even touched—they
must be felt with the heart.

HELEN KELLER

Swag: decorative gatherings of fabric at both sides of shade

Plain fold: a flat surface appearance with seams every few inches

Relaxed: a loose pool of fabric at the end of the shade

Banded: a decorative trim or banding on either side of shade

Tie: the fabric is collected at the end by ties

Win-Win Options for Awkward Windows

Most homes have a window that is tricky to treat with drapes or shades. Here are some suggestions that may solve your troubles.

C H A L L E N G E: Windows Bunched into Corners

Solutions:

— Frame both windows with long panels. Use clip-on rings to decrease bulkiness.

— Try two sets of panels with Roman shades. Separate the curtain rods and use Roman or woven shades.

— Frame the windows using one curtain rod. Use an elbow connector and two panels in the corner to feel plush.

stationary window

solution

CHALLENGE: Bay Windows

Solutions:

— Use bay-window specific drapery rods or separate small rods across each window.

— Put draperies straight across the wall outside of the bay window.

— If draperies don't work well, use a Roman shade.

Bay Window

Solution 1

CHALLENGE: Vaulted Ceilings and High Windows

Solutions:

— Use an extra-large curtain rod above the lower windows with Roman shades for added style and greater control of light.

— For drama, hang your curtain rod closer to the ceiling, even on very tall walls.

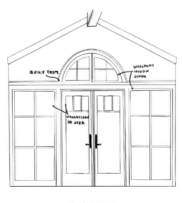

Vaulted Ceiling

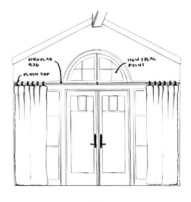

Solution

CHALLENGE: Paned Exterior Doors

Solutions:

— Use a single panel and pull across as needed, or use a panel on either side of the door.

— Install a Roman shade or apply a solar shade directly to the door.

stationary window

solution

CHALLENGE: Small, Tucked-Away Windows and Dormer Windows

Solutions:

— Roman shades are a good option for small windows.

— Anchor a window with a desk, window seat, or other substantial piece placed beneath it.

— Try valances for small windows above a sink and swing-arm rods for basement windows.

C H A L L E N G E : Wall of Windows

Solution: Try small groupings of high-hung drapery. This allows for sunshine to get through but still has a polished, designed look.

C H A L L E N G E : Odd-Sized windows

Solution: Try cordless shades and add a valance to elongate the look of window.

C H A L L E N G E : Stair Windows

Solution: Avoid hanging drapes over stair windows. Instead, opt for cordless Roman shades.

Some windows can be left elegantly bare. If a home has beautiful decorative molding around the windows, let them sing solo, especially if you are merging two design styles. For example, one home had gorgeous black window frames in the dining room, and we left them bare and bold and spectacular.

W I N D O W S   O F   O P P O R T U N I T Y

Here are some lovely, unexpected options that open your home to illumination.

— *Skylights.* Add a patch of needed light in a dark hallway, bathroom, loft, bedroom, or office with skylights. Technological options allow for automatic shading, opening and closing, and more. Smaller tube skylights can be installed relatively affordably.

— *Windows in doors and above doorways.* Install pocket doors or French doors with windows between rooms to allow light to flow between spaces.

— *Uniquely shaped windows.* Think outside the box and consider windows that are round, octagons, crescents, or arcs.

— *Cutouts.* Openings in walls between rooms act like windows and permit light to stream between rooms.

— *Shutters.* These work best with farmhouse and cottage styles. They can block light and the view, so keep that in mind.

Let There Be Light...Fixtures

After you have explored how to maximize natural light, evaluate the functional and accent lighting to illuminate your design and personal needs. Consider where and why you need it. Stroll through your rooms and create a list. For example: by bedsides for reading, above desks or the kitchen island for tasks, and permanent or accent fixtures in most rooms for multiuse. Once you see all the amazing choices available to you in fixtures, you'll be glad you know what you need so you don't get lost. Five sconces and no primary light in a room will eventually drive you nuts. Create a combo from the main types of lighting.

Ambient. This general lighting includes recessed and can lights, track lighting, sconces, chandeliers, and pendant lights. Soffit lighting is placed beneath structural overhangs outdoors and indoors. This can provide drama, function, and glowing beauty. If your ceilings are too low for a chandelier and you're a chandelier kind of gal, get an attractive semiflush mount ceiling light to let your personality shine in your space.

Task lighting. These fixtures facilitate tasks like cooking, reading, and working at computers. Don't let the word "task" fool you— these options are very fun to shop for when you are ready to add personal touches. They include table lamps, pendant lights, and under-cabinet lighting.

Accent lighting. This is used to highlight an object or area of architectural interest. For example, picture lighting showcases artwork. Tight on your budget or just want to skip electrical work? Install a battery-operated LED picture light. Our son Asher has one in his room above his giant chalkboard.

You'll want your choices to work together smoothly and not be overdone. Nobody wants their living room lit up like a supermarket. Here's a common formula for lighting a room.

ROOM LENGTH X ROOM WIDTH X 1.5 = WATTAGE REQUIRED

You may want more or less depending on the function of the room.

Spotlight Your Style

Emerging beauty is never more evident than when function marries style. You have your list of lighting needs . . . now explore the options that suit the look, mood, and style you desire. For example, I'm fond of pendants, chandeliers, sconces, and clever accent lighting.

Take risks and go for something a little outside your norm. These can end up being the favorite parts of your home. Why? Because your house doesn't look like your girlfriend's house, and you have now mixed in an element that adds the perfect amount of interest and balance to create a truly bespoke look.

Lighting choices allow you to be bold and honor your look. Instead of going with a typical pendant in a kitchen, for example, try an oversized pendant with design flair to add some drama and va-va-voom. The perfect touch of chic.

In an open-concept home, you may be tempted to get a set of lights that all match. Instead, let one light be the main focus and

then pick one or two more styles that are interesting and unique to complement it and add originality to the space.

———

I've established how much I love light, right? The power of light cannot be overstated. Look around your home and notice those missed opportunities to brighten the sacred place you call home.

WALK-THROUGH MOMENT

Which room in your house will be most improved with increased natural light and well-chosen fixture lighting? Pay attention to the shift in the room's beauty and mood.

NINE

INSPIRE THE MOOD

Think back to grade school, when you were given a blank piece of paper and an array of paint colors. You felt joy, right? You probably didn't overthink whether it was okay to paint a purple cat in a red tree. You surveyed the color options, made choices, and created whatever felt right to you. Somewhere on the way to adulthood and home ownership, a lot of us lose that freedom. Maybe we forgot how to give ourselves permission to trust what we like and make choices accordingly.

Reclaim that joy so you don't miss out on one of the most powerful expressions of beauty. Color will bring your personality into your home and honor the mood you want to evoke. And paint is one of the most affordable and impactful ways to express your color palette. Don't be afraid of something that is easily changeable, especially when the payoff of falling in love with your color choice is spectacular.

And you *will* fall in love.

Daydream in Color

Even if you don't color code your files or arrange your closet in rainbow order, you are drawn to certain hues. In color speak, the hue is the basic color. Designers and artists also play a lot with the value of a color (degree of lightness or darkness) and the intensity (degree of purity). You are responding to those when you reach for the brilliant sapphire-blue scarf or your gaze lands on the rich copper in a mosaic vase.

Notice the emotions that rise when you look at certain colors. Pay attention to what you are drawn to when you look at the color strips in the paint department or a hue in its natural habitat. Those blush-pink peonies might fill you with calm and nostalgia. The verdant green moss on the backyard tree might give your mind a rush of energy and joy.

Take inventory of the colors you surround yourself with. Are they working for you? If your walls are the same beige the builder chose for you fifteen years ago, you are probably ready for change. See which colors you are drawn to for furniture or accessories. I have clients who show me their absolute favorite treasure, and I'll point out the colors that attract them to that piece are not found elsewhere in their home. They know the shades that soothe or inspire them but haven't fully invited them to into their spaces.

Color, like light, is a foundational source of beauty and meaning in our homes.

Mood and Inspiration

An established mood in your home creates a longer-term emotional response than a first-impression feeling. It can evoke a deep calm or whisk you away to a high-energy state. Every object and color choice you bring into a room will either add to your space or take

COLOR, LIKE LIGHT, IS A FOUNDATIONAL SOURCE OF BEAUTY AND MEANING IN OUR HOMES.

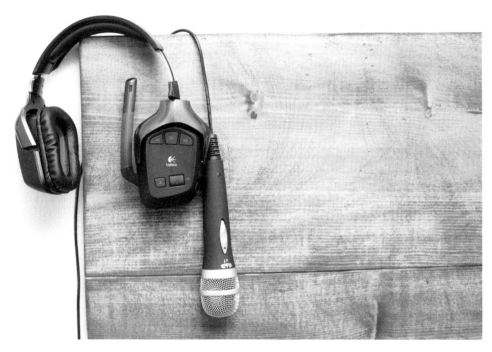

away from it. That is why it's so important to clearly define your voice for your home.

The mood I want my home to evoke has several layers. I want the first impression to be peaceful, welcoming, and comfortable. Next I wanted to pepper in uniqueness and a few quirky moments. Your home is the primary place you have freedom to create and reflect what matters most to you.

Do you want a bedroom to be calm and peaceful? Consider gray-blue or beige. Greige is the gray and beige combo that is all the rage. Greens and blues that are soft are also tranquil. Interested in a dramatic or moody dining room, study, or guest bedroom? A deep emerald green or charcoal gray is nice. Imagine a hallway with a gallery wall against a dark color. Amazing.

COLOR CONFIDENCE

These tips for various stages of the process will build your color confidence and help you get the most impact of color in your space:

— The 60-30-10 rule creates a color scheme with ease. Use 60 percent of your space for the dominant main color, 30 percent for the secondary color, and 10 percent for the accent color.

— A neutral gray will appear warm when placed on a blue background and cool when placed on a red background. Now you know why finding the perfect gray can be so difficult!

— Warm colors tend to advance or feel closer, and cool colors recede or appear further. For example, a long, narrow room can be "widened" by painting the side walls with a light, cool color and painting the end wall with a darker, warmer color. A high ceiling can be "lowered" by painting it a darker color.

— Avoid using a stark white in a room without windows because the tone will feel flat and sterile. Use undertones of beige, gray, or cream.

Inspire
the Mood

—Consider whether the color of one wall will clash with an adjoining wall or any trim. Yellow undertones and cream undertones can look dingy. Hold the sample of the wall color up to baseboards, doorframes, and crown molding to check.

—In an open-concept space, you can change color at a natural breaking point. For example, if a wall has a ninety-degree turn from the kitchen to the living room, you can shift colors there.

—A sample against a white wall will appear darker than it is, and that can trick you into choosing a shade lighter than you want. Compare your sample against a sofa, a fabric, or even flooring for a better perspective.

—When painting over a dark color base, use a primer. Quality all-in-one paints with primer are helpful. If the base you're covering is particularly saturated, use two coats of primer. That costs less than multiple coats of paint!

—Paint last when you can. If you are installing new floors or purchasing significant furniture pieces, get those elements in your home and then decide which wall color works best.

Before You Watch Paint Dry

The painting process takes patience...even before you are standing in front of a bedroom wall with your trim taped, a roller in hand, and a gallon of a rich hue you adore. Choosing the right paint takes some time and research. This also helps you avoid paint panic.

Two bits of advice: Don't rush. And don't take too long and end up frozen. This guidance will help you find the sweet spot between being thorough and being overwhelmed.

PLAY WITH THE OPTIONS

You know those color strips that make you seize up with indecision? Those can be your greatest tools in learning about the undertones of colors. Look at all the colors carefully and notice the dominant, underlying color as the shade gets darker on the strip. This will

Beauty is a gift of God.

ARISTOTLE

help you steer clear of undertones of blue, green, purple, and so on if that's not what you're going for. Seeing the undertones is a lot harder when the color is standing alone.

SAMPLE AND IMAGINE

Don't purchase gallons of paint based on a choice made from a magazine photo or a blog post. Photographers, printers, and computer monitors have too many filters to show the true color. Start with Pinterest and Houzz photos to narrow your list, and then look at the color decks and color samples at home and near the furniture and accessories you love. (Some companies even offer sample sticker panels you can place on the wall.)

Once a sample is on the wall, look at it in all lighting scenarios. Daylight shows the truest color, incandescent lighting brings out warm tones and yellows, and fluorescent lighting casts a sometimes harsh, blue tone. Because of this, a bold color might be too bright and overpowering when used on all the walls, but it might be effective when used as an accent wall with indirect light.

EXPERIMENT, EVALUATE, AND ADJUST

Ask for your color to be mixed at both a lighter percent of the formula and a higher, darker percent. Request paint for your color at 70 percent, as is, and at 120 percent. A color you like but aren't quite sure about can become "the one" when you see it in a slightly different concentration. Put this idea to use in a bedroom. Paint the walls at the normal formula and then use a 50 percent version for the ceiling. This way you don't have to go in search of the perfect lighter color. The ideal variation is done in a jiffy.

Start small. Experiment with a powder room, bathroom, small hallway, or accent wall. Pick a small area to paint and let it dry. That way you can see your results sooner and decide whether you love it or need to make changes.

CONTRAST AND COMPLEMENT

Contrast is the secret ingredient that gives memorable spaces their impact. When used correctly, this foundational design principle can add a huge dose of visual interest to your interiors while simultaneously pulling them together.

Try to choose an element or color or texture that complements and contrasts its surroundings. When I help clients update their exterior color palette and curb appeal, 90 percent of the time the trim color needs a new coat of paint. Instead of suggesting it be repainted in the safe beige it was, I might draw their attention to the dark charcoal flecks in the brick exterior and suggest it as a beautiful accent color for the trim. The result is a home that feels fresh and interesting.

Urbanology Designs had a client who was remodeling a 1905 bungalow. The owner wanted some color in her very outdated kitchen. We agreed the cabinets were the very best place to get a bold punch of personality and contrast! We went with a dark green (Foxhall Green by Sherman Williams). We contrasted it with a white square tile backsplash to ensure the focus stayed right where we wanted it. This green provided the moody nostalgic look we were going for. The result was simple and stunning.

CONSIDER COLOR WITHOUT PAINT

Wallcoverings offer endless possibilities with texture, contemporary design, and every color and pattern under the sun. This could be the perfect way to stamp your individual style on a room and add drama and color without paint.

Wallpaper is no longer the shiny, plastic stuff that dominated the eighties. (Don't get me started on the apple-basket border we had in our kitchen when I was a kid.) New digital printing technology offers prints that are oversized and whimsical. The colors are rich and bright. The fabrics are textured and sometimes three dimensional. Best of all, new adhesives make installation and removal easy.

Consider the beauty benefits of wallpaper for a dining room or bedroom that is ready for an unexpected touch of design and dimension!

Be Brave! Create a Moment.

Enjoy the freedom to include your personality. Embrace opportunity to create drama with a bold accent wall, a contrasting trim, or an unexpected paint detail. Creating these intentional and sensational moments in a home is my absolute favorite thing in the world to do for a client (or to empower them to do).

If you create a cool, bright wall for your artwork, you aren't overcommitting or overextending, and it will likely become one of your favorite spaces. Look at your home with new eyes. This gives us a starting place to brainstorm and plan those special moments of beauty and delight. Here are some moments I created to embrace my desire for layers and whimsy.

My living room is white, light, and airy. I wanted the perfect spot for the unexpected and dramatic to play out. The answer was a high, angled wall that you can see only after you've entered the room. I affixed thin wood slats to the wall for geometric interest and texture, and then I painted it in Hague Blue by Farrow & Ball, which is rich and deep without showing off.

My son Asher's room is designed primarily with neutral colors. I painted the closet door a deep hunter green and added a porcelain white doorknob for contrast. It is just the right creative moment for this small space.

The lower three-quarters of the walls in Maddie and Lily's room are painted with a blush-pink color and a lighter shade above it. The horizontal line where the blush ends is continuous around the room.

In our dining room, the dark blue paint goes a little more than halfway up the wall and also covers the door and baseboards for a unique look.

My Favorites

Here are some of my favorite paint colors to recommend, especially to those who love Urbanology Designs' signature modern, nostalgic look. Even if your style is different from ours, you'll likely discover a few complementary colors in this lineup.

FAVORITE NEUTRALS

Simply White by Benjamin Moore

Classic Gray by Benjamin Moore

Ultra Pure White by Behr

All White by Farrow & Ball

Wevet by Farrow & Ball

Pure White by Sherwin Williams

FAVORITE ACCENTS

Hague Blue by Farrow & Ball

Off Black by Farrow & Ball

Calico Blue (dark green) by Benjamin Moore

Stiffkey Blue by Farrow & Ball

Caviar Black by Sherwin Williams

Submarine Gray (blue-green) by Behr

FAVORITE TRIM

Decorator's White by Benjamin Moore

White Wisp by Benjamin Moore

Off Black by Farrow & Ball

Alabaster by Sherwin Williams

Metropolitan by Benjamin Moore

Shoji White by Sherwin Williams

FAVORITE FINISHES

Matte is my favorite sheen for its rich finish that doesn't reflect imperfections. If you need a finish that's easier to clean, choose eggshell. For baseboards and moldings, consider semigloss. Satin enamel has a lower sheen and is still highly durable for cabinets. Farrow & Ball makes a matte-finish cabinet paint that is beautiful and durable.

———

Colors enrich our experiences, evoke moods and memories, and nurture the hearts and days of people in our lives. Give yourself permission to experiment so you can immerse yourself in shades of beauty.

WALK-THROUGH MOMENT

What colors are you drawn to? Which of these suits the mood and style you want now? Decide where to create a painted moment of whimsy or refreshment in your home. Are you feeling brave enough to pick up a brush?

PART IV

GATHER BEAUTY

TEN

ENJOY THE HUNT

FURNITURE AND SHOPPING

The quest for the ideal piece of furniture has likely ignited joy and frustration for centuries. One challenge that becomes a blessing (I promise) when redesigning your home is accepting the fact that you don't have the space or the budget to get everything you want—and more importantly, that not everything you like is what you want in your home. Limits motivate and guide you to choose the right pieces, the best pieces. (There's the silver lining to that budget of yours!)

Even if a person has vast financial resources and a home with more square footage than the local concert hall, they eventually must make the three choices everyone does: What stays? What goes? What is added?

To make your best choices for your home and before you remove or buy furniture, look at your

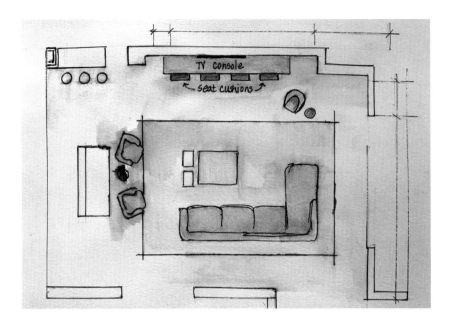

home's physical boundaries—room sizes and the floor plan. From there you can choose furniture that serves and elevates your daily life.

Mapping Spaces

If your finger is about to hit enter to order a new couch online, I'll be the friend who says "Wait!" This temporary pause of your retail adrenaline rush will save you lots of headaches and help you plan for a home you'll love. You need to do a couple things before you buy.

If you've ever stubbed your toe on your bed frame or dealt with a room that drives you crazy, there's a good chance the culprit is a poorly planned space. Good design incorporates form and dimension. A room should feel safe, comfortable, and welcoming. You can plan the perfect mission and mood for your home, but if the areas are not designed intentionally, you'll miss the mark. So here we go. You'll need paper, painter's tape, and a tape measure. Class is in session. If you can do this in an emptied room, all the better. If not, do your best to maneuver around the furniture.

—Make a drawing of the floor plan and use this paper to record measurements.

LIMITS
MOTIVATE AND
GUIDE YOU
TO CHOOSE
THE RIGHT
PIECES, THE
BEST PIECES.
(THERE'S THE
SILVER LINING
TO THAT
BUDGET OF
YOURS!)

— Measure and record the size and the spaces between windows and walls, windowsills and the floor, and so on.

— With tape, mark on the floor the shapes and sizes of the furniture you plan to include. Tape task zones to preserve those spaces.

— Evaluate the space as you look at the taped outlines and zones. You may discover that the full-sized sofa you want for your living room will fit after all. See, waiting is a good thing!

What Stays, What Goes?

Some designers like to work with all new pieces. Not me. I advise clients to shop their house first. Using what you have means you'll have a bigger budget for what you need and want. And recognizing your gems allows you to incorporate your favorite pieces in every stage of your redesign plans.

Personal and sentimental value matters. If a piece has significant meaning because of who gave it to you or where you purchased it, make a space for it. Just be sure to do the hard work of evaluating what you have and making sure you don't get stuck with too many objects. When you choose to keep only the elements that are most important to you, you will enjoy and value them because they won't be competing with a ton of less meaningful pieces.

Even though I partner with brands I love, my family will tell you I still swoon over the pieces I built or repurposed when we had almost nothing. In our living room, we have a set of bare wood shelves that I built from tree branches. It cost me nothing except the afternoon it took to build it, and after several years and a decent amount of design experience, I still consider this one of my favorite pieces.

The simplest tactics often deliver the major wows.

I also made our dining table. Five years ago I sourced the reclaimed wood from a building that was more than a hundred years old. I drove out to the country with my girlfriend and my circular saw to cut the wood on site. The wood was so dense my saw started smoking. I piled the wood in the back of the pickup truck and headed home.

Since then, I haven't yet seen a table I would swap for this piece, which represents the inspiration, elbow grease, and love I needed to complete it. And now that I have precious memories of my family gathered around it for meals, it is an absolute treasure.

———

If you still have items you are unsure about, let's take a closer look. Each stage of this process will enhance the end result. Here are a few questions to ask about each piece: Have you used it in the past six months for anything other than a surface area to gather piles? If the piece doesn't serve the style or function of a main room, does it offer the wow factor in another room? Is it unique enough to create a special moment that highlights your personality? If someone borrowed this item and fell in love with it, would you want it back? Is it a piece you want to pass down to children or other family?

If the answers are no, it is time to say goodbye.

Now that you've selected what to keep and what to pass along, you can focus on what to add to your home.

The Hunt

I have friends whose smiles grow wide with bliss when they consider shopping. And I have other friends or clients whose eyes grow wide with overwhelm and are more likely to get stuck than get shopping.

For both personalities, I offer priorities as the key to happy choices. If we return to our theme of what matters most, we can know when and on what to spend money or save money. Substantial pieces and those you want to pass on to the next generation are worth the investment. This category includes a sofa, a dining table, a chair that will get a lot of use, and perhaps your bed frame. Save money on other furnishings, such as side tables. I strongly recommend that you buy quality furnishings, even for the less expensive pieces.

CHOOSE QUALITY

As a teen, I shared a room with my sister Laura. We saved up a year's worth of earnings from babysitting and other odd jobs because we had our hearts set on matching twin sleigh bed and dresser sets. With our hard-earned money, we strolled into Haverty's, a furniture store, and bought our dream bedroom set in dark cherry wood. We asked for a discount if we paid cash—something we surely learned from our dad. When our furniture arrived, we arranged and rearranged everything just so. We were in heaven.

In hindsight, I realize I was following a principle that matters to me still—shop for quality and durability on important pieces. I kept those beds a long time. After my sister passed away and I adopted her young son, it was meaningful to use one of the twins for his first big-boy bed. Our younger brother inherited the other bed, and he has it to this day.

According to the EPA website, the amount of furniture discarded in the United States rises every year and accounts for millions of tons of waste. To avoid needless waste, I encourage my clients to source responsibly.

For something to be durable, it must weather the wear and tear. Pieces made of synthetic materials—MDF, particleboard, or plywood—have the advantage of being cheap and stylish, but they wear down quickly. For the items in your home that get the most traffic, you want real materials. A kitchen table made of hardwood will better handle your kids squirming around as they do their homework, make arts and crafts, and drop their forks and knives yet again. The nicks and marks will become memories, not blemishes.

CONSIDER CUSTOM

Custom pieces have a story, they are unique, and they support local communities or individual artisans. Custom pieces might be higher priced than retail options, but they are often cost effective when you consider keeping them for decades! This falls under the category of "you get what you pay for." Think beyond the cost to the benefits.

Beauty as we feel it is something indescribable: What it is or what it means can never be said.

GEORGE SANTAYANA

You can personalize a piece and have control of important factors. Handpick fabrics and wood, and decide with the craftsman which special touches will elevate your piece of furniture to a piece of art that offers function, comfort, and beauty. If you have an exceptionally large living room or an awkward layout, instead of spending months on dead-end searches for a piece of proper scale, you can have one designed for you.

If you're interested in hiring someone to build a custom-crafted piece, ask for recommendations on your neighborhood Facebook page. Watch for artisan fairs too. The Dallas–Fort Worth area hosts these each year, and I come across amazing artisans. If planning all the details is overwhelming for you—there *are* a lot of measurements and decisions—work with an interior designer to create the design and manage its fabrication.

A custom treasure is bespoke and reflects your individual style sensibilities. When each piece is a statement unique to you, your home feels polished and put together from the ground up.

MAGNIFY YOUR PURCHASE POWER

—Create a roadmap with information, plans, and patience to get what you love.

—Do your research. See what you like and know what your space and your budget can support comfortably. And read online reviews of items and retail sources.

—Don't impulse buy. Don't get it unless you know right where it will go and that it fits your plan for the beauty of your home.

—Wait for true love. I had a coffee-table design in mind for two years before I found someone who made what I envisioned. Don't buy just to buy. See what is out there. Go with a girlfriend to flea markets every couple of weeks and keep looking till you fall in love.

—Measure twice, buy once. Be sure you are looking at those measurements when you make your purchase.

— Not all the pretty things! Stick to the budget and choose wisely. It stops being fun if you have financial stress or use your entire budget on an impulse buy.

— Get samples. If the retailer offers fabric samples, request the color you're interested in as well as one color lighter and one color darker.

— Shop vintage stores and online sources. It is inspiring to survey pieces in designs you aren't seeing in your everyday searches. I love scouting options at Chairish.com.

— Include your spouse. Trust me. See what matters to them. For example, a client loved the look of slim arms on a sofa, and her husband wanted a broad armrest. The solution? A couch with a slim arm and a substantial side pillow for width.

— Consider the oft-forgotten furniture pieces for added personality: poufs, ottomans and stools, floor mirrors, and floor baskets and chests for storage.

The Quest for the Dream Sofa

Couches are the most pursued and most perplexing furniture choice. As a designer I've seen and evaluated them by the hundreds. It appears you get comfort and durability or style and elegance, but rarely everything. Which is why my team and I at Urbanology Designs eventually created custom pieces—the Santa Clara Sofa and the Newport Loveseat. Here are some elemental factors that will help you find happily-ever-after furniture.

— *Durability of the fabric.* We think of this after a child has spilled grape juice on the cushion! Ask for a performance fabric to protect against stains and spills. (If you have the piece already, hire a company to seal furniture or drapes with a protectant.)

— *Scale and size.* A big couch in a small space will feel cramped and a small one in a big space will be awkward. Typical sofa size is 84 inches. Consider a 72-inch sofa in a small living room and

a 96-inch sofa for spacious rooms. A general rule is that a sofa should not occupy the entire length of a wall—leave at least 18 inches of space on either side of the sofa. If any family member is tall, consider a deep cushion for comfort and fit.

— *Comfort and structure.* Look for a cushion with a foam core in a down wrap for structure and softness. Select a sofa with only one or two seat cushions for an elegant look.

— *Visual weight.* If the sofa base goes all the way to the floor with stubby or nonvisible legs, it will feel heavy. If you have heavy-looking armchairs, choose a sofa with visible legs for an airy look.

— *Contrast.* Don't worry about matching the flooring hardwood to the wood of furniture legs. Tones too yellow, orange, or red are not advised. Beyond that, there's a good chance the contrast will create a nice complementary mix. Limit to two or three wood variations.

A thoughtfully curated room will bring you immense delight and will be a blessing for your family and guests. Function and attractiveness can partner together. Hold fast to your goal of creating a place of beauty for real life.

WALK-THROUGH MOMENT

What piece of furniture would enhance the aesthetics and comfort of your real life? Do you have your eye on something?

ELEVEN

CREATE BALANCE AND INTEREST

MIX, TEXTURE, LAYER

love what you've done!" Anyone who has remodeled or redesigned their home is of course pleased when they hear this from visiting friends. But I will let you in on a little secret: My heart soars when people walk into a space, look around, smile, and say it's a room they want to spend more time in.

Beauty emerges in a home shaped by intentional choices. Balance and interest invite us to interact with a space using our senses. A part of your brain sounds off with joy because it wants you to savor the sight of the room as a whole as well as individual moments created with forethought. Another part of the brain chimes with delight and compels you to reach out and touch the lush fabric of the chair, the woven threads of the tapestry, or the contrast between the smooth oak floor and the chunky wool rug.

THERE IS

NOTHING

MATCHY-

MATCHY

ABOUT

REAL LIFE,

AND THERE

SHOULDN'T

BE ANYTHING

MATCHY-

MATCHY

ABOUT REAL

BEAUTY.

The most beautiful visual moments in your home will be created with contrast, just as some of the most beautiful parts of your life will be shaped by change and emotionally layered experiences. Look at one room or one season of life closely, and you'll see the truth in this. There is nothing matchy-matchy about real life, and there shouldn't be anything matchy-matchy about real beauty.

To guide the creation of functional and fascinating spaces, try this winning formula: mix, texture, layer. The result is a home that invites you, your family, and your friends to engage with the environment and elements of each room. We'll explore how to do this with arrangements, mixed materials, and natural elements in a way that enhances your style and space.

Arrangements for Dimension and Interest

A well-designed room is welcoming and functional. The rich tangible layers and engaging visual layers add depth and spark interest.

When you find that sweet spot where function meets beauty in your space, you do more than just earn other people's praise—even though it feels really good when others enjoy your house. Your home becomes the place where you happily wind down with ease in the evening or spend the rare and precious lazy morning off. With a little advance planning, you can create a room that welcomes and engages and even inspires you and others.

—*Consider your point of entry.* I like to position the sofa (the biggest, most obstructive piece in the room) to the left or the right of the entry point of the room. Why? I don't love walking into the back of a sofa. I like living rooms to be open and inviting.

—*Establish the room's focal point.* Do you want to capture a beautiful view? Do you need a comfortable place to see the TV? Do you have a fireplace that would make a nice focal point? Your choice determines where to place furniture and at what angles.

—*Know the flow.* Allow adequate space between furniture pieces for proper traffic flow. Think through how a room will be used.

(Tip: Place your coffee table sixteen to eighteen inches from your sofa for comfortable flow and accessibility.)

—*Let furniture size guide you to a cohesive layout.* A large sofa should not be shoved in a corner, but given prominence. Smaller seating options, like backless benches, poufs, stools, and ottomans can be placed in front of the fireplace or a coffee table without blocking the view. When choosing a sectional, the chaise portion should not extend more than halfway across the room. (Tip: For small-scale furniture, visit antique shops. Historically, rooms and homes were not as big as they are today, so vintage furniture tends to be smaller.)

—*Balance the arrangement.* Distribute larger pieces of furniture rather than clustering them in one area. Then balance with visually lighter pieces. For example, if you have two massive armchairs, consider a sofa with exposed legs to give the room a sense of visual lightness.

—*Arrange a natural conversation area.* Avoid pushing furniture against the walls; instead, pull furniture close enough to create easy conversation. In a very large space, consider creating multiple seating areas grouped so that guests are within ten feet of each other. One of my favorite room layouts is two full size sofas facing each other, a backless bench on one end and two armchairs on the opposite. This is not ideal for viewing a TV... maybe that is why I like it so much!

—*Unify the space with a rug.* Go big. If you can, ground your furniture with all four legs on the rug. The next-best scenario is to place the front legs of your furniture on your rug. Your room will benefit from the softness, texture, and layers the rug provides.

—*Add texture to create balance and harmony.* A room is texturized with rugs, smooth wood finishes, fuzzy pillows, throw blankets, hewn wood beams, linen window treatments, sleek glass and metals, and hard and soft finishes.

— *Bring life into your space.* Highlight a view of a garden or a majestic oak tree. Or bring greenery into your home. (I have lots of suggestions for you a bit later.) Don't have a green thumb? Consider a faux olive tree. Today's faux greenery is not the plastic fern of yesteryear.

— *Access the power of accessories.* This may be the most blissful of all beautification endeavors. Accessories personalize your space and create the warm welcome to come in and stay awhile and the intriguing invitation to take in details that inform and delight. Carefully curated books, objects from your travels, woven baskets, sculptural vases, vintage candle holders, pillows, mirrors, artwork, and artisan treasures bring the much-needed finishing touches to any home! Resist filling your room with stuff—invite pieces that are special to you or carry a story. We'll have fun exploring how to style spaces with accessories in the next chapter.

Mix Metals to Maximize Beauty

Be brave, my friend. Take the risk of mixing metals and fabrics to get a look that is original and rich.

Let's start with metals. So many people stick to just having one kind of metal finish in a room or even their entire home because they've heard that's just the way it's done. I say, free yourself up and enjoy the loveliness of variety. Begin by selecting the item you love the most, whether it's a matte-black faucet or a brass light fixture. Then select another item that matches or coordinates closely with the finish of that first metal.

Next, layer in a different accent metal (or two) to complete the look. A good rule of thumb to use at least two different metals but no more than three.

For example, a kitchen's visual texture can benefit from variety, such as brass light fixtures paired with chrome faucets and layered with matte-black cabinet hardware. That's a win. Experiment in a bathroom or a home office to start. There are many great combinations. Here are a few to try:

BRUSHED BRASS + NICKEL OR POLISHED CHROME

AGED BRASS + POLISHED CHROME

MATTE BLACK + AGED BRASS + SATIN NICKEL

POLISHED BRASS + SATIN NICKEL + OIL-RUBBED BRONZE

OIL-RUBBED BRONZE + POLISHED NICKEL + AGED BRASS

MATTE BLACK + POLISHED CHROME

Mixing metals creates a curated, designed look rather than the less interesting outcome when buying a collection at one store.

Combine Cloth to Create Interest

Now we weave our way to fabrics. (Insert happy dancing.) Mixing textiles is an affordable and creative way to up the interest in your space. Here are a few combos that work well together:

— *Wool + cotton.* For example, a wool rug and cotton pillows mix textures and create visual and tactile interest from the moment a person enters a room.

— *Silk + linen.* Silk curtains in a room with a linen upholstered chair or throw blanket present the contrast of refined and formal with material that is visually light.

— *Jute + cotton.* The jute or sisal rug layered with a flat-weave cotton rug provides a lovely contrasting layer. The juxtaposition of an organic, more rugged material with the softness of cotton is quite attractive.

— *Linen + wool.* Light and airy linen curtains paired with a chunky wool throw blanket offer you loads of softness and the bonus of different textures complementing one another.

— *Velvet + satin.* Ahh...a smooth velvet sofa with satin pillows is indulgence at its best. Both fabrics will catch the light and create their own unique mood. Pairing these offers richness and elegance.

Style really comes down to
what makes you feel good.

ALEXANDRA STODDARD

When you add patterns to the mix, you get even more character and dimension. Use at least three patterns in a room to create interest and depth. It's important to vary the scale of your patterns so you are not mixing all small or large patterns, which would overwhelm the eye.

When sprinkling different patterns into your window treatments, rugs, pillows, or an upholstered chair, distribute the patterns evenly throughout the room to present balance. Patterns can also be tonal, with very subtle visual. Patterns are usually considered colorful, but they can also be monochromatic. A rug of one color with varied pile length and thickness offers a beautiful but simple monochrome pattern and texture.

Rugs Do It All

Rugs have benefits aplenty: warmth, style, character, texture, contrast, coverage...and they help create cohesive spaces as well as home-defining unexpected moments. A rug doesn't have to be pattern-heavy to make a statement, but it's a fun way to go bold, especially if your furniture is simple. One of the most important considerations for your rug selection is that its design doesn't compete with the furniture around it.

Choose the best material, size, and shape for your room. You have endless options for rug colors and designs, and you have wonderful selections for a rug's weave and material. When making a final decision, order samples or see the rug in person to make sure your choice looks the same as it does on screen.

The right rug will bring beautiful texture, layers, and balance into a space, anchoring all the movable pieces to make the room feel complete, interesting, and fabulous.

WEAVE

— *Flat weave.* My favorite pick. Thinly woven. No pile. Often reversible.

— *Hand knotted.* Another favorite. Created on a loom. Rich in texture, soft, imperfect.

- *Machine made.* Created on an electric loom. Very uniform. Serged edges are common.

- *Hand tufted.* Individual threads pushed through a canvas and then looped and cut. Tends to shed. Soft.

- *Hand hooked.* Small loops hooked through canvas. Creates a circle-like pattern. Light shedding.

- *Shag.* Woven rug with a thick or fluffy pile. Variety of lengths and textures.

MATERIAL

- *Wool.* Best for durability and softness. Great for high traffic. Naturally repels stains and water.

- *Cotton.* Soft but not plush. Normally machine washable.

- *Natural fiber.* Strong and durable. Stains easily. Coarse to the touch. Great texture.

- *Synthetic.* Durable. Great for high traffic. Can feel artificial.

- *Silk.* Luxury. Best softness and luster. Suited for low-traffic areas.

- *Hides.* Smooth and thin. Makes a statement. Great for layering.

Don't forget to search for vintage rugs. There are amazing ones of such great quality. Moroccan and oriental rugs add depth and character.

Nature's Decor

Bring in the green to add dimension, texture, color, and life to large spaces and intimate nooks. Plants are natural miracle workers wherever they go with their brightening, uplifting, air-purifying, beautiful little leafy selves. Start envisioning how to add life to your life.

- *Create the perfect "shelfie."* Add plants aside other decorative pieces to your shelves. Small potted plants are perfect for bookshelves, floating shelves, or media shelves.

- *Remember the unexpected places.* Consider placing small plants on a bathroom windowsill or on steps. A staggered

presentation of three plants draws the eye. Place a tall potted plant at the end of a hallway, perhaps overlapping a piece of art on the wall. Set plants in corners of your dining room for depth. Adorn side tables and nightstands with sprigs of life.

— *Let them take center stage!* Plants work exceptionally well as centerpieces, whether on a kitchen island, a dining table, or a coffee table.

— *Inspire task stations.* Make tasks more enjoyable by placing a small plant on a kitchen counter, a bathroom sink area, or in the laundry room.

— *Introduce nature to kids' rooms.* Give your children the gift of nature in their bedrooms and play spaces. Assign plants' watering and caretaking to their young owners.

———

I cannot emphasize this enough—a whole, lovely life and home will have variation, depth, meaning, complex moments, smooth areas, transitions, and layers. When your home reflects this, you will feel the peace that only an intentional, authentic sanctuary can offer.

WALK-THROUGH MOMENT

Which textures compel you to reach out and touch them? Which of those will you introduce into a room's new design? What is one layer you will add for interest?

TWELVE

DESIGN BEAUTIFUL MOMENTS

A home is a place you live in, not just look at. You aren't curating a museum! So my advice is not to create displays, but to design authentic moments.

When you design a home that reflects your truth, inspiration follows. That's why from the depths of my heart, I want you to know what interests you and the unique something that you bring to the world. Styling your home is not about showing off your things; it's about living in beauty and enjoying what you have...sharing what you love.

Rediscover What You Love

Sometimes I walk into a room in our house and realize that one of the kids has moved an object. I'll look at it for a bit and realize I am seeing new beauty in its new home. I admit I often return the item to its original shelf, but occasionally I like it in

STYLING
YOUR HOME
IS NOT ABOUT
SHOWING OFF
YOUR THINGS;
IT'S ABOUT
LIVING IN
BEAUTY AND
ENJOYING
WHAT YOU
HAVE…
SHARING WHAT
YOU LOVE.

the different setting. I enjoy the way I respond to it in a new space or at a different angle, so I leave it there. I even move items in clients' homes to help them see the pieces in a new light and maybe even transform objects into treasures.

We create our best moments in our home when we place items intentionally.

Have you purchased, discovered, or been given something that evokes an emotion in you? Where is it right now? Consider giving it a new spot. Make it a focal point on a shelf or another surface. Make it a centerpiece. Give it an entire surface or wall to invite others to engage with it and see it for the gem that you do.

Go through your house room by room and notice what you love. Then find it the perfect home within your home. Atop a small stack of stones, place the shell your son found when he was six and saw the ocean for the first time. Remove the quilt from your grandmother's cedar chest and drape it on a favorite reading chair. On the white mantel, place the floral porcelain teapot you bought at an antique market for your birthday. Hang that painting from your grandfather or grandmother.

This is styling from the heart.

Invent a Special First-Impression Entryway

Often the entry becomes a convenient catchall for junk mail and those last-second necessities, like sunglasses and car keys. Of course, that is only convenient until you are tripping over shoes or digging through piles of mail, which impacts the space's function as well as your home's first impression.

Big or small, your entryway can become a memorable moment in your home. Invest a little time and money into some furniture and/or accessories, and you can really make a statement.

— *Work with what you have.* If you don't have space for a standard-size console table, mount a shelf or two to the wall and free up space underneath for shoes and bags.

— *Expand a space with mirrors.* Add a mirror to reflect light. You can make a space look larger, and you can also do that quick check for spinach in your teeth before you face the world.

— *Decide what gets to hang out.* Add a few peg hooks on the wall to create consistent spots for coats, hats, or scarves. Position a few for little ones so they can grab or hang their bags and outerwear without help.

— *Make the most of a larger entry.* Create a stunning vignette with this functional area. Set it apart from the rest of the home with a dramatic color for the backdrop or a material for the flooring and the wall.

— *Have a seat.* Add a bench that suits your style and the mood of your home. Bench hunting is very fun...so many styles and eras to consider!

— *Style special touches to serve your family.* A ladder is a clever place to hang or drape scarves, totes, decorative signs, or small baskets to keep keys, sunglasses, and other out-the-door necessities close at hand but out of sight.

Showcase What You Love on Shelves

Trust me, your shelves long to be turned into inviting moments! They are tired of gathering dust instead of beauty, collecting your odds and ends instead of actual collections, or remaining bare because you are reluctant to bare your personality.

Before you start on your shelves, edit out what you don't need or like. Take an afternoon to declutter and make room to showcase your accessories and curated pieces that have meaning and reflect your interests and passions.

— *Create a backdrop.* If your shelving is large enough, use artwork, wallpaper, a wooden box, or a plate to serve as your backdrop and to draw in your eye with rich layers.

— *Feature a variety show.* Shelves are home for many of your favorite vintage objects, greenery, sculptures, vessels, collections, and perhaps even lighting. Mix up the textures, sizes, styles, and tones, but stay within that color palette so it doesn't look like a thrift store. Choose two or three colors to accent and draw attention. To avoid overdoing it, try staying in one or two design styles (farmhouse, vintage, midcentury modern, and so on).

— *Highlight the beauty of books.* Whether you have first editions or an eclectic library of favorite reads, stack your books both vertically and horizontally and pepper the colors around evenly for a collected look. For an eye-catching display, remove the jackets of hardcovers and reveal the gorgeous array of colors in book bindings. I often group books by the color of their spine.

— *Keep smaller objects contained.* Collections or trinkets or candles are organized and appealing when grouped together. For example, gather items in a tall glass vase or corral shorter item collections on a tray or another attractive, shallow container.

— *Pay attention to scale.* Notice how I mention this for many design topics? A variety of heights, shapes, and volumes will add interest to your display. Achieve balance by alternating the sizes and colors.

— *Use that top shelf.* Don't miss out on this great place to display large collection pieces. Vintage fans? Globes? Tree branches or other natural elements? The possibilities are endless!

Plan a Gallery Wall that Wows

Artwork should embrace your personality and give the space a thoughtful representation of you. When done well, a gallery wall is breathtaking. Don't rush to create a gallery wall to fill the space; instead, be thoughtful and intentional to choose pieces you really love.

— Don't commit too fast. Lay out a grid on your floor using a roll of craft paper, and trace out the art frames. Or make paper cutouts the size of each piece of art and practice placement with tape on the wall before you commit with a hammer and nails. This allows you to play around with the perfect placement.

— Start with your largest art pieces and work around them. They will be your anchors. Consider both horizontal and vertical placement.

— For the best final result, upgrade to a glare-resistant glass or museum-quality glass to improve visibility and protect your artwork.

— When hanging pieces, don't "eye it." Measure and plan for space between each frame—four inches is a good guide. Center the grouping within the available wall space or over the piece of furniture below it.

— Create a cohesive color palette. Treat a grouping of pictures as a single unit by choosing colors that go together and contrast. Choose a few primary colors and pepper in accent colors. On the other hand . . .

— . . . an eclectic gallery wall can brim with variety and color. Don't be afraid to mix up your frames. Chunky vintage frames and streamlined modern ones can still play well with each other. Stick to two or three styles and colors of frames and matting so your gallery wall doesn't feel cluttered. It is also fun to add in some non-framed art, like antlers or pieces with depth and character.

FOCAL-POINT ARTWORK

Not ready for a gallery wall in your living room? Place a significant piece of artwork above a sofa for a timeless look. The trick is to choose the right piece. Maybe it is one you commissioned, found on an important trip, or fell in love with at the flea market.

When displaying a single large piece of art, the center of the picture should be at eye level, approximately sixty inches from the

One's destination is never a place but rather a new way of looking at things.

HENRY MILLER

floor. Leave a three- to six-inch gap between the top of a sofa and the bottom of the picture frame and four to eight inches of room from a tabletop. Use a level to make sure art is straight—especially if it is hanging on more than one nail. Finally, position pictures away from direct light and high humidity to make the color and paper last for years to come.

Sofa, So Good—Make It Inviting

With a few styling tricks, you can highlight your dream sofa or significantly enhance your "good enough for now" couch to dramatically improve the overall look of your room.

— *Start with a blank canvas.* Whether it is covered in white cotton, gray linen, navy velvet, or light tan leather, a neutral sofa is a decor classic and allows for a variety of decor combinations. New sofas usually come with a set of matchy-matchy pillows. You may want to throw those pillows in the giveaway pile and swap for something more unique for a personal look.

— *Begin your layers.* An odd number of pillows makes for the most natural, inviting arrangement: three for smaller sofas and five for larger ones. Start with a pair of neutral-toned pillows to create a versatile foundation for the rest of your arrangement. For the base pillows, choose a texture that plays against your sofa in an interesting way. I love how slightly rough linen looks against buttery leather. Velvet or wool would be equally lovely.

— *Play with colors, patterns, and scale.* Now for the fun part! Pick a pair of square pillows—either the same size as your first layer or a little smaller—in a color and pattern you love. Try for one sofa color and two or three pillow colors. And the general rule for patterns is to mix prints in different scales or keep your prints in the same color family.

— *Add more layers.* With your pillow party complete, you can focus on elements like throw blankets. I like to go with the texture of a big chunky throw. Drape a throw over the arm of the sofa or the middle of the back.

— *Consider adding a rug at the base of the sofa.* Choose a color that complements the pillows. Leave a little breathing room between the sofa and the wall.

Create Beauty in Unexpected Places

Still unsure where and what to style? You can start anywhere. You can create the most enjoyable moments in your home in unexpected places. Here are a few ideas to get you brainstorming for your own spaces.

The area at the foot of your bed can become a mini-conversation area or peaceful wind-down space. Try two chairs that face each other, a bench, or a chaise lounge and a chunky throw.

Ends of hallways can be a uniquely painted moment and a spot for a striking vignette with a chest and artwork.

Make work a pleasure. Your tasks will be more enjoyable if you style your office space. Include comfort elements, such as a cozy chaise. Choose stylish functional pieces, like a vintage floor lamp.

After putting easily accessible shelves and baskets in my son Asher's closet, I created an artwork gallery wall. It's a feature he and I can keep changing. Unexpected beauty is a joy no matter your age.

Moments in the kitchen are easily formed with a piece of artwork or a stylish lighting source, such as a wall sconce. We even redesigned and styled our second pantry with a moody blue/green paint called Dark Night by Sherwin-Williams. Then we put in maple floors and covered the ceiling in a solid maple sheet and wired in the beautiful flush-mount fixture from CB2. We added a roller cart, a double shelf with hooks, and narrow shelves for canned goods. A warm Turkish rug adds an unexpected touch of warmth. If you have a quirky little space like this that needs a little help, take a weekend to tackle it and exercise your creative muscles.

I had the privilege of helping design the bunk room in Goldie's House, a home for girls rescued from sex trafficking through the

organization Unlikely Heroes. I wanted to create a personal, unexpected moment for each of the girls. The question was, how do we achieve this in a shared space? After brainstorming, we built ledges and shelves for each bunk to house a girl's treasures and belongings. We added healing beauty with commissioned pieces by a local artist. And we designed a cozy seating area to nurture recovery and to allow these girls a space to just be teens—chatting with friends, dreaming about the future, or stressing over homework projects!

Style Your Unique Moment

When I travel, my favorite activity is visiting local flea markets or artisan shops. On a business trip to Los Angeles with one of my designer girlfriends, we spent all day going from shop to shop. I wasn't set to buy anything; I was happy to soak it all in. Then I laid eyes on a special vintage rug, and I knew it needed a home (mine)! I also knew it would become part of what I call a "unique moment." These are special nooks, rooms, spaces, or vignettes that engage, delight, or even surprise those who encounter them.

The already amazing rug became a unique moment when I worked with my local frame shop to custom frame and matte my new treasure. I chose a thin white frame with a white matte for a fresh, modern look. This will have a special place in a new bungalow we are building in our backyard.

Whether it's a prized collection or a hobby you need space to pursue, what you love doesn't have to come second. I'm known for breaking the rules. I love to add something unexpected or what I call "a little touch of weird or unexpected;" choosing pieces that are inspiring and meaningful to my clients. Here are some examples of this.

Above my bed I have an old painting of a ship on the ocean that I found at an antique store. The edges of the image are curled, so the paper does not rest flat under the frame. But I loved its drama and imperfections the minute I saw it.

Bare shelves can be beautiful. I intentionally styled a bookshelf with lots of negative space. Unique objects and unexpected art become focal points as they are displayed in the otherwise naked vignette.

Asher's giant oversized chalkboard is an unexpected moment that plays up and emphasizes scale and creativity. Not to mention it is incredibly fun to use for notes and drawings!

Urbanology Designs' project in West Flower Mound, Texas needed something special for the living room. In this case an intriguing "must-have" emerged during the process—a unique sculptural console table. Our client would either absolutely love it or point us toward the door. Taking the risk on a slightly "out there" piece paid off! Not only did our client love it, it absolutely made the room!

Design a Moment to Share

The most important moments we create in our homes may very well be those we enjoy temporarily with others. Designing a tablescape for a gathering is an opportunity to express your style and to delight others with beauty. The holidays inspire us, but don't miss the other countless opportunities to decorate your table throughout the year. Serving others sparks my greatest creative energy! Here are ways to consistently create a tablescape that is personal and welcoming every time.

— *Start with a foundational fabric.* Lay the groundwork for a beautiful display. Choose a runner, a tablecloth and runner combo, or a piece that you don't typically think of for your table, such as a blanket or a scarf.

— *Layer as you mix scale, pattern, and texture.* Start with the largest item in the middle, such as a centerpiece, and work your way out as you display decorative and primary serving pieces. Instead of a single centerpiece, you can have a display of mixed items. For example, place a short decorative or natural item alongside taller glass candle holders or vases to vary scale. I like

to include at least one patterned element, whether that is the plates, napkins, or the runner. If all are of the same color family, it looks amazing.

— *Showcase natural elements.* Shopping from the great outdoors offers endless assortments. At holidays I've used dried magnolia leaves mixed with various sizes of pumpkins, greenery, and acorns. Integrate succulents with cut flowers. Or use a green garland or herbs wrapped in twine—this looks especially nice tied to the dinner napkins. These add warmth and visual interest.

— *Add a surprise.* Handwrite your own place cards for a personal touch. Your guests will sense that the spot was prepared just for them. I also like to place a special little something on each plate: a ramekin holding a roll wrapped in butcher paper, a bunch of rosemary or lavender wrapped in twine, or a personalized verse or quote on a pretty notecard.

———

The visual and experiential moments you create in your home will speak to the hearts of those who live there and who visit. When you express your personality, plumb lines, and priorities in cozy nooks and designed special touches, you communicate more than your style...you design the gift of authentic beauty.

WALK·THROUGH MOMENT

Take a moment to plan a moment! Choose a place to add character, a quirky surprise, or unique beauty. Do a special walk-through—tour each room and express gratitude for it. Let yourself experience the blessing of beauty.

Design Beautiful
Moments

YOUR SHARED BEAUTY

s our journey comes to a close, I imagine gathering around the table in my mind. We are sitting together, sharing our experiences and the lessons we've learned. Which walk-through moment helped move you from unsure to unstoppable? How have your mission and personality emerged in the look and comfort of your home?

I pour freshly brewed tea into our large, white ceramic mugs, and we let the steam rise. We rest in the fellowship and our mutual love of home. We ease into deeper conversation about what paths have led us to this moment. Since I envision us seated at the first table I ever built and the one that brings together the people I love, I ask the question my family uses as a conversation appetizer before every dinner: What is your high? What is your low?

You and I know that life is filled with both. The challenges and the times of overcoming. The detours and the daring leaps forward. The sorrows and the surprising joys. Through every high and every low, beauty is woven, strengthened, magnified, and illuminated to reflect your unique story. That, my friend, is the story that shines in your home and in every choice you make with intention. Your beauty is shared in every welcoming room, sunlit corner, and inviting arrangement.

You are doing it, my creative and worthy friend.

From the moment you walked through the open door of this experience, you have been dreaming, envisioning, planning, and transforming the place you call home. You are making life richer and better. Because you open your heart and home, many others will walk through your front door and feel the love and the life you've cultivated with care. They will be welcomed because you create and share beauty with intention and faith—they will be blessed because you create beauty by design.

BEAUTY
BY DESIGN

These resources and retailers (and many more) come together to form my candy store! They offer treats and treasures and delights galore. These are places you can go to research, dream, plan, and maybe even purchase. But believe me, you don't have to buy anything to be fed and inspired by beautiful images, ideas, and styles.

FURNITURE

The Citizenry	Lostline	Target
Lulu and Georgia	Design Within Reach	Article
Horne Modern	Clad Home	Amsterdam Modern
Dwell Studio	CB2	Horchow
Serena and Lily	Anthropologie	Room and Board
AllModern	West Elm	Moss
HD Buttercup	Crate and Barrel	Ferm Living

VINTAGE

Chairish	1stDibs	OfferUp
Sunbeam Vintage	Etsy	Vogt Auction

LIGHTING

Rejuvenation	Katy Skelton	Blue Print Lighting
Human Home	Allied Maker	Circa
Apparatus	Cedar and Moss	Worsley Lighting
	Schoolhouse Electric	

RUGS

Trout House Rugs	Rejuvenation
Plush Rugs	The Rug Company
Lulu and Georgia	Flor
Dash and Albert	Ruggable

WALLPAPER

Walnut Wallpaper	Murals Wallpaper
Hygge & West	Livette's Wallpaper
Farrow & Ball	Anthropologie
Cavern Home	

WALL DECALS

Urbanwalls

Rocky Mountain Wall Decals

Chasing Paper

CHILDREN'S WALLPAPER

Little Hands Wallpaper

Livette's Wallpaper

DECORATIVE PILLOWS

Kesslyr Dean	One Affirmation
Arianna Belle	Design Public
Kaekoo	Tonic Living
Perigold	

ART

Holly Addi	Artfully Walls
Claire Ritchie	Sugarlift
Minted	MQuan (Michelle Quan
Markus Walters	Studio)

WALL TEXTILES

Vita Boheme Studio   Block Shop Textiles

FABRICS

Susan Connor New York   Mod Green Pod

Calico Corners   KUFRI

BEDDING

Parachute   Matteo Los Angeles

Snowe   Dwell Studio

Brooklinen   Magic Linen

Olatz

POTTERY/CERAMICS

Kendall Davis Clay   Charlotte Moss

Natan Moss   Heath Ceramics

THrō Ceramics   Spartan Shop

WINDOW TREATMENTS

The Shade Store

Smith & Noble

FLOORING

Burlington Design Gallery	Mohawk
Exquisite Surfaces	Zia Tile
Paris Ceramics	Bedrosians Tile & Stone

ACCESSORIES

Gifted	Heath Ceramics	Parachute Home
Gathre	Zara Home	CB2
Two Tree Studios	Chairish	H&M Home
Circle and Line Design	Fishs Eddy	Alder & Company
FS Objects	John Derian Company	Food 52
TableArt	Kaufmann Mercantile	Ferm Living

PAINT BRANDS

Farrow & Ball	Sherwin-Williams
Benjamin Moore	Dunn Edwards

ACKNOWLEDGMENTS

Special thanks to...

My dear friend Krissy. This book would not have come to fruition without your wisdom, guidance, and belief that there was a story that needed to be shared. After endless nights and zillions of edits to capture the heart of the home, I knew you were right. I'll never forget your beautiful contribution.

Sonali Chanchani and Frank Weimann of Folio Literary Management for seeing the value of my message and passion.

Harvest House Publishers for partnering with me to share my heart with readers and create something truly beautiful.

My design friends and colleagues who have encouraged me along the way. I admire and look up to you, Linda, Julia, Nicole, Staci, Ruthie, and Kim.

The artisans who make our work possible and bring it to life. Jason, Collin, Sammi, Brandi, M&M, Chad, and Brent, your commitment to your craft will be appreciated for years to come.

My clients. It is a privilege to come into your homes and help you create the beauty you deserve.

The Interior Design Society for creating and fostering authentic community among designers worldwide.

Those who trust in the LORD
will find new strength. . . .
They will run and not grow weary.
They will walk and not faint.

ISAIAH 40:31 NLT

Father God, no words are sufficient to thank you and fully recognize you for your incredible work in my life. I have experienced the deepest sorrows and the deepest joys with you by my side. You have taught me to have a trust that is without borders. You mended my broken heart many times over and have filled my sails with fresh wind and lifted me to new heights. When I did not believe in myself, you believed in me. I am forever and always yours. I am your girl, and I love you with every ounce of my heart.

ABOUT GINGER

Ginger Curtis is the owner and founder of Urbanology Designs, the home design firm she founded in 2015, which is based in the Dallas–Fort Worth metropolitan market.

Ginger won the First Place Designer of the Year Award for 2016, 2017, 2018, 2019, and 2020 from the Interior Designer Society. She was a finalist for HGTV's 2017 and 2018 "Faces of Design" awards and has won the Best of Customer Service award from Houzz.com, the world's biggest website and online community for home design, as well as Houzz's "Best of Design" award—a distinction given to the top 3 percent of interior designers in the world.

She was chosen as a top-25 designer in Texas by Amara Living, top-10 interior designer in Dallas, and a winner of the Fort Worth "Fort Worthy" Business award for two consecutive years. Urbanology Designs was selected to design a unique restaurant for one of the new Market by Macy's stores in the Dallas–Fort Worth area.

Ginger, her team, and their creative design work have been featured in more than fifty print and online publications and were featured in and on the book *Architecture Today: Interior Design*.

As a breast cancer survivor and mother of five children (including a ten-year-old leukemia survivor), Ginger is passionate about serving several cancer research and awareness organizations, including the Leukemia & Lymphoma Society. She received the Legacy award from Unlikely Heroes, an organization that rescues children out of the global sex trafficking industry. She is also a mentor to women interior designers and business owners.

Ginger lives with her husband, Eric, and their children in the Dallas–Fort Worth area.

The quotation of Isaiah 40:31 is taken from the Holy Bible, New Living Translation, copyright © 1996, 2004, 2015 by Tyndale House Foundation. Used by permission of Tyndale House Publishers, Inc., Carol Stream, Illinois 60188. All rights reserved.

The quotation of Romans 8:28 is taken from the Holy Bible, New International Version®, NIV®. Copyright © 1973, 1978, 1984, 2011 by Biblica, Inc.® Used by permission. All rights reserved worldwide.

Cover and interior design by Faceout Studio

Cover photo by Matti Gresham
Photographs on pages 31, 33, 46, 50, 53, 104, 147, 212 © Ginger Curtis
Photographs on pages 1, 5, 6, 8, 10, 14, 55, 57, 62, 66, 69, 70, 73, 108, 110, 116, 133, 172, 175, 176, 179, 181, 185, 187, 208, 211 © Matti Gresham
Photographs on pages 13, 17, 27, 28, 54, 56, 74, 77, 78, 81, 82, 118, 121, 134, 139, 140, 155, 158, 161, 166, 169, 170, 224 © Sesha Smith – Convey Studios
Photographs on pages 52, 107, 144, 188, 191, 192, 195, 198, 201, 202, 205, 206 © Mary Hafner
Photographs on pages 20, 24, 88, 91, 92, 96, 99, 222 © Jerry Turnbow
Photographs on pages 34, 38, 41, 43, 44, 114 © Hunter Coon
Photographs on pages 58, 148, 150, 151, 152 © Norman and Young Real Estate Media
Photographs on pages 51, 136 © DM Photography
Photograph on page 221 © Kristina Avila

All photographs used by permission.

М® is a federally registered trademark of the Hawkins Children's LLC. Harvest House Publishers, Inc. is the exclusive licensee of the trademark.

Beauty by Design
Copyright © 2021 by Ginger Curtis
Published by Harvest House Publishers
Eugene, Oregon 97408

www.harvesthousepublishers.com

ISBN 978-0-7369-8224-5 (hardcover)
ISBN 978-0-7369-8225-2 (eBook)

Library of Congress Control number: 2020948471

Printed in China

21 22 23 24 25 26 27 28 29 / RDS–FO / 10 9 8 7 6 5 4 3 2 1